* breakthrough thinking
using creativity to solve problems

CREATIVE BUSINESS SOLUTIONS

*breakthrough thinking

using creativity to solve problems nick souter

artwork by guy billout

ILEX

First published in the United Kingdom in 2007 by

I L E X

The Old Candlemakers
West Street
Lewes
East Sussex BN7 2NZ
www.ilex-press.com

Copyright © 2007 The Ilex Press Limited

Publisher: Alastair Campbell
Creative Director: Peter Bridgewater
Associate Publisher: Robin Pearson
Editorial Director: Tom Mugridge
Editor: Ben Renow-Clarke
Art Director: Julie Weir
Designer: Jonathan Raimes
Design Assistant: Kate Haynes

Artwork © Guy Billout

British Library Cataloguing-in-Publication Data
A catalogue record for this book is available from
the British Library

ISBN 10: 1-905814-13-5
ISBN 13: 978-1-905814-13-8

For more information on this title, go to:
www.web-linked.com/bideuk

Printed and bound in China

CD-ROM Contents

There are five interactive software tools on the
attached CD-ROM.

They are:

1. **The Emotional Compass**. This will help
   you find out exactly where you are in the
   Ideascape.
2. **Fishing**. This tool introduces random words
   as bait for new ideas so that you can escape
   the Ocean.
3. **Backtracking**. This tool will help you
   abandon a mirage and find a new way out
   of the Desert.
4. **Sidewalking**. This tool will get you out of
   the City by simplifying the problem with
   an analogy.
5. **Trailblazing**. This tool will reorganize the
   information you already have to find a new
   path out of the Forest.

contents

1. How to use this book

Creativity is our competitive edge.

If we are to continue ruling this planet while allowing technology to take over the workforce, we can reassure ourselves with the thought that machines and computers will always be our slaves. They will do our bidding, as and when we tell them.

Why? Because, unlike us, they lack imagination.

For the most part, that is the main difference between a human's brain and a computer's brain.

But what if that advantage were to prove fragile and not endure? For decades, Science Fiction writers have reveled in the horror of what would happen if machines learned to think independently and develop emotions. Would they use their ubiquity, their networked communications and their superhuman strength to overthrow us?

Would they "terminate" us?

Ray Kurzweil, in his book *The Age of Spiritual Machines*, looks at how the exponential development of processing power, when harnessed to new computing concepts such as Artificial Intelligence and Neural Networking, could put us in the position of being intellectual inferiors by the year 2021.

That's a mere 15 years. Not that long at all—many of us will live to see it happen. But we shouldn't panic. In the meantime, what John C. Lilley called the "human bio-computer" will remain the only mechanism on Earth that can think creatively and develop new and original ideas. Which means we get to determine the future and the role that technology will play.

For the moment at least, the best computer available is the one sitting in your head.

Which begs the question, do you know how to use it?

My guess is that, as with the computer that sits on your desk, you've mastered the basic functions, learned a few shortcuts, and know how to get things done without worrying too much about the way it works. That's how most of us treat computers. We know they contain a vast untapped potential, a multitude of menus, dialog boxes and functions that we do not understand or use.

And so it is with the Brain. If neuroscience is to be believed, none of us access much more than 10% of our entire brain's capacity. Einstein included.

But in our defense, we get very little help and encouragement.

Brains don't come with a manual. We are not sent free, downloadable upgrades for our operating system. And we receive only limited instruction throughout our education. We study and develop the mental software programs needed for memory, logic, reason, analysis, and calculation.

Creative thinking is rarely on the curriculum.

As a result, many highly intelligent people—and by that I mean people who have learned to use their mental computers and can access lots of useful information —will claim that they are not at all creative.

But I disagree. I don't think that is true at all.

What they are really saying, I believe, is that they haven't yet developed or been shown how to find an application for the limitless power of their imaginations.

Hence the concept of this book: cerebral software.

Breakthrough Thinking is like a software application designed for your brain.

Its purpose is to give your mind greater creative functionality.
(To complete this digital metaphor, let me say that I see your Brain as the CPU or Central Processing Unit that does all the work, and your Mind as the VDU or Visual Display Unit where you select and input information and then later review the output.)

Chapter 2 takes a look at why Creative Thinking and Innovation have become personal and corporate imperatives in recent years. In business life these competencies have gone from being "nice to have" to "must-have." Careers and companies now depend on them.

With that in mind, Chapter 3 explores the resistance some people have to acknowledging their creative thinking potential. If you doubt yourself and doubt your creativity, don't skip this chapter—it might help you overcome a painful and self-fulfilling prejudice. We're all creative if we give ourselves the chance.

Chapter 4 attacks that ubiquitous metaphor for creative paralysis, "The Box," and establishes six principles that can help us break out of it.

And Chapter 5 investigates the notion of a "creative process." Does such a resource exist or is this a contradiction in terms?

Great ideas rarely come out of thin air.

Usually, they occur when a problem has been examined inside and out and then clearly articulated. Chapter 6 looks at how to interrogate, and, if necessary, restate a problem to make sure that the ideation process starts off on the right foot and generates useful and practical solutions.

Chapters 7, 8, and 9 are the Cerebral Software Manual. Here you'll find detailed instructions on how to use the Creative Compass and the mental tools and widgets that make the Breakthrough Thinking system work. If you're the sort of person who always turns to the Quick Start section of a manual, go straight to these pages.

Finally, we'll turn our attention from generating ideas to nurturing ideas. New concepts are dangerously fragile.

A thoughtless remark or just the shrug of a shoulder can crush a brilliant thought before it has the chance to develop and become an innovative idea.

Chapter 10 establishes some principles and behaviors that can inspire and build a Creative Culture—a workplace environment that protects and nurtures ideas until their true value can be understood and appreciated.

Breakthrough Thinking is a simple and methodical approach to creativity, and it becomes more intuitive the more you use it.

It started life as a concept I called "Right brain thinking for left brain people"—a system for reorganizing our thoughts when we find ourselves creatively "stuck."

It then developed into a metaphor—a software program for the mind, our own internal computer.

And from the metaphor it became a reality. Attached to this book you'll find a CD-ROM that contains the Creative Compass and four Breakthrough Thinking tools in interactive software form. Load them onto your computer and they'll work as your digital thinking partners.

From concept, to metaphor, to reality.

Such is the power of creative thinking.

2. Accelerated evolution

Some two and a half millennia ago, the Greek philosopher Heraclitus made an observation that has been translated and rephrased throughout history and which usually reaches us in these words:

"Change is the only constant."

The years have proved him to be right and, consistent with his thinking, the speed of change has also continued to change. It gets faster. Never slower.

Most of us, even within the perspective of our short stay on the planet, have the uneasy sense that the pace of life is starting to speed far beyond our control—certainly beyond our comfort zone.

Entire industries and technologies are now dedicated to kicking us into a higher gear to help us keep up. Virtually all activity in developed countries is caught in the grip of this accelerated evolution.

We eat faster, we communicate faster, we travel faster, we shop faster, we study and learn faster, we work faster….

The list goes on. Quite simply, we live faster.

The food supply chain is an interesting case in point. At the cost of meeting our nutritional needs, the food industry has dedicated itself to saving us time in the preparation process.

What may have started with the quaint image of American families sitting down to TV dinners has become a norm of freeze-dried "just-add-water" magic powder meals, pre-prepared dishes that are "nuked" in microwave ovens, cooked food that we drive-thru to collect or which someone else drives to our house and delivers.

And while we may be chewing and swallowing at the same speed as our grandparents (although I suspect they appreciated their food in a more leisurely fashion), we're now doing that chewing "on the run."

During my years in advertising I worked as a Creative Director on the Kellogg's account and saw the development of their "convenience food" category. (Convenience in this context meaning time-saving.) Thanks to their culinary skills and technology, breakfast is changing from a sit-down family affair to a granola bar eaten on the bus while preparing for a day in the office.

And ironically, this is presented to the consumer as a healthy option.

But as well as preparing and eating our food faster, we can now shop for it faster. The successful development of the supermarket isn't simply explained by the bulk buying that facilitates competitive pricing. Supermarkets save more than money, they save time. One-stop shopping— food, household goods, clothing, dry cleaning, banking, gas, pharmaceuticals, alcohol, you name it. It's all under one roof.

As if to prove the value of the concept, the supermarkets grew into the malls—those massive, suburban cathedrals of consumerism where we worship the power of the dollar and save even more time in the process.

But that's still not fast enough.

And so we have supermarkets that offer online shopping. One click and they'll deliver. They'll even save your list of regular purchases so that you don't have to waste time checking the boxes again next week.

Online services, the Internet and development of information and communication technology are perhaps the most potent accelerants to affect our everyday life.

Gone are the days of licking a stamp and hoping your carefully worded letter makes the last post. (A letter that, without the benefit of a word processor, would have taken an inordinately long time to write.)

Today, global communication is virtually instant. An email reaches its target in seconds and yet, it would appear, there is still time to be saved. So what do we do? We write it faster. We dispense with salutations, proper grammar, spelling, and, sometimes, capital letters. If we know the recipient and the recipient knows us, we may even omit signing our names because our identity will be clearly established in the "sender" field at the top of our message.

These new communication protocols are reinforced and encouraged by the development of SMS or "texting."

C U @ 7 o/s K-Mart :)

trips off the thumbs faster than "See you at seven o'clock outside K-Mart. Love, Nick."

True, this form of abbreviation is also a response to the difficulty and frustration of manipulating the small numbers that are now standard on most mobile phones.

But the handset itself is a powerful emblem of how the march of technology is accelerating. A mobile phone is pretty much obsolete from the day you buy it. Tomorrow's model will have a plethora of new features and functions designed to increase your ability to interact with the world with a more immediate, and therefore time-saving, response.

It's much the same with computers. Unless they are your hobby, the likelihood is that you haven't learned to use your current software before it's upgraded to a new release. But that frustration is a small price to pay when one considers how much faster they let us work, calculate, research, study, learn, and communicate.

In just three short decades, the PC has turbocharged our lives.

And yet we want it to be faster still. That's why we upgrade. More power in the processor, more speed on the desktop. The same with downloads—we want faster, broader bandwidth in our cable networks. What seemed a miracle of modern computing last year is now frustrating and tediously slow.

Unfortunately, the faster we develop new technology, the faster it becomes redundant, out of date. Try selling a year-old computer. It's junk. Your best hope is that someone on eBay takes it off your hands and spares you the pain of watching it gather dust somewhere and serve as a reminder of just what a short-term investment it proved to be.

One persistent problem with technology is that it is impossible to predict the course its development will take.

The future contains too many unpredictable variables, any one of which might alter the trajectory of a new invention.

When Thomas Savery invented the steam engine in 1698 his sole purpose was to pump the water out of Cornish mines. Could he have guessed that 116 years later his contraption would be strapped to wheels and emerge as the world's first railway locomotive? And would George Stephenson, in 1829, have had the gall to call his locomotive "The Rocket" if he could have envisaged the TGV network that now connects London, Paris, Brussels, and Lille at speeds of up to 190 mph (300 km/h)?

It's much the same story in aviation. In 1903 Wilbur Wright would have laughed at the suggestion that something the size of an Airbus A380 could one day lift off the ground. But from today's vantage point, it doesn't seem remotely surprising.

What once seemed impossible now seems overdue.

And so it is we find ourselves rushing with ever-increasing speed into a blurred and uncertain future. And that's just the view from within our limited experience and perspective. If we stand farther back, the picture becomes far more dramatic.

It's hard to imagine our place in the history of time. The challenge is overwhelming. However, Carl Sagan's "Cosmic Calendar" gives a remarkably graphic sense of where we fit in and how fast our world is changing.

In Sagan's concept we collapse the entire history of the universe into a single calendar year and then see on what dates significant events occur. January 1 begins with a Big Bang but then the year gets off to a pretty slow start. The Milky Way doesn't make an appearance until May 1 and life, that most precious of things, doesn't actually appear until September 25.

There's a high point on November 1 with the invention of sex. (We should establish a national holiday, even though it was only microorganisms involved.)

But it's not until December that Mother Nature really gets cracking. We have oxygen from the beginning of the month and life starts to take on forms we would recognize today. The first worms invade the earth on December 16 and fish start swimming on December 19. Christmas Day marks the start of the Permian period and briefly dinosaurs rule the world. But, given the pace of evolution by this stage of the proceedings, they don't last long. They're gone by December 28.

It's on the last day, December 31, that the real frenzy of evolution begins. Humans show up around 10:30 in the evening. By 11:00 they are wielding tools and by quarter to midnight they have learned the art of making fire.

Thereafter, nothing can hold them back. In the last minute of the year we develop agriculture, art, the alphabet, law, cities, war, physics, mathematics, religion, and science, and undertake global voyages of discovery. And yet it is in the very last second of the very last minute of December 31 that we truly surpass ourselves. In that blink of an eye, science and technology enable us to create a global culture, take our first tentative steps into space, develop medicines to protect our species, and a weapon that gives us the means to destroy it.

Phew! It really makes you wonder what is going to happen in the next second or two.

How are we to survive this headlong rush into the future? We have only one option. We must adapt and evolve. It's just that every year we are going to have to learn to do that faster.

And that is where creativity plays its vital role.

The process by which we adapt to changing circumstances is essentially a creative one.

There is no better place to study this than in nature, where evolution is revealed to be a continuous act of creativity on the part of those species that evade extinction. Look at Sagan's calendar and you'll see that the creatures that didn't make it to New Year's Eve were those that lacked the ability to change.

Arthur Koestler's 1971 book, *The Case of the Midwife Toad*, creates a detective story out of the rivalry between the supporters of Darwin's belief in Natural Selection and those of Paul Kammerer's Theory of Acquired Characteristics. Central to the plot is the evolutionary behavior of the midwife toad.

Kammerer, who committed suicide in 1926 after being falsely accused of faking evidence, bred many generations of these toads in captivity and proved that they developed new physical characteristics in order to ensure the survival of their species. These toads mate in water. But the success rate of their procreative behavior was compromised by the fact that the male would often slide off his partner before the act was complete. Mother Nature intervened to spare these creatures with a simple and creative solution. The female toads developed mating pads on the backs of their legs which afforded the males a firm grip and made sure that their hard work was not wasted.

And so the species survived and thrived.

Nature is teeming with examples of how many different creatures and organisms have used the creative-mutative process of change to avoid extinction.

One of Nature's finest achievements is the wing. For much of our natural history, wings did not exist (at least 11 months of Sagan's year). Now there are many varieties of insect and bird who can hunt for food more effectively while avoiding their predators thanks to this wonderful invention.

Clearly, it was born of necessity. And as Plato said, "Necessity is the mother of invention." But necessity doesn't just shape the future of the organisms we study in nature. It affects the organisms we have created in the world of business and commerce—organisms we call companies and corporations.

If these species are to survive and thrive, they too will have to think creatively and adapt accordingly. And they will have to do that faster every year. In their world, frequently described as a "jungle," the process is most commonly referred to as Innovation.

For the purpose of this book, I'll define Innovation as "Creativity that has found a useful purpose"—one that will improve a company's systems, products, or services. Ultimately, it will increase its profits and improve the wellbeing of the company's employees and customers.

One only has to read the daily press to note that Innovation has become the buzzword and Holy Grail of senior management in corporate life.

Bill Ford in *Time* magazine recently said, "Innovation will save this company."

A. G. Laffley, current head of Procter & Gamble, has invested heavily to transform his process-driven juggernaut of a company into an organization that has an agility that only a creative-thinking culture can develop.

Pick up a copy of Unilever's company brochure and you'll see a very similar philosophy in action. In fact, you can pick up any company brochure or trawl through their website and you'll find the CEO emphasizing their belief in innovation.

This trend is a necessary response to a very real threat of extinction.

Eric Beinhocker, a Senior Fellow at McKinsey's Global Institute and author of *The Origin of Wealth*, draws attention to a study of the 500 companies listed in the S&P (Standard and Poor) Index when it was first published in 1957. Only 74 of them survived until 1997. In other words, over 40 years, 85% of the original S&P 500 had disappeared from the face of the earth. Extinct.

It would seem that size and a history of success are no guarantee of survival.

Paul Ormerod, author of *Why Most Things Fail*, elaborates further:

"The probability of failure, or extinction, is known to be highest when the company is first formed. It then falls away rapidly. After a short period of time, just two or three years, the probability of failure in any period of time is then unrelated to the age of the firm." He goes on to say:

"Perhaps more surprisingly, there seems to be very little connection between the size of a firm and its probability of survival in any given period."

British retailer Marks & Spencer would be a good example of this misfortune. Years of innovation and diversification made it the iconic high street chainstore in the UK. In the mid-90s it was the largest clothing retailer in the country as well as operating a multi-billion pound food empire, with a third line of business in homewares. In 1997 it became the first British retailer to declare a pre-tax profit of over £1 billion. And then, quite suddenly, its evolution stalled and the company plunged into crisis. Today, in 2007, it is recovering but is now less than one-quarter of the size of the UK's biggest and most profitable retailer, Tesco.

The history of corporate life is littered with such stories of near or total extinction. They all serve to underpin the argument that innovation is the only means of escaping such a fate.

Jennifer Chatman, a professor of the Haas School of Business at the University of California, confirms the positive influence of an innovation-based culture on a firm's long-term sustainability.

Her research found that, over an 11-year span, the revenues for firms that have a culture that is strategically relevant and strong in innovation outperformed those firms that don't by 682% to 166%. Furthermore,

the net income for firms that are focused on innovation increased by 756% compared to 1% for those who had not developed a culture and philosophy of thinking creatively.

In an environment where every company is striving to maintain a competitive edge, a 756 to 1 advantage has to be a convincing argument in favor of innovative thinking.

Richard Foster and Sarah Kaplan further support these conclusions in their challenging and contentious book, *Creative Destruction*.

Foster and Kaplan are a Senior Partner and Innovation Specialist from McKinsey and Company. Drawing on research the company has conducted on more than 1,000 corporations in 15 industries over a 36-year period, they observe that corporations that are founded on the Built-to-Last principle actually underperform the market by a significant amount.

They attribute this in part to the accelerating pace of change that has led us into what Peter Drucker calls the Age of Discontinuity. In this environment, capital markets and corporations operate under widely differing principles.

Markets are built on the assumption of discontinuity. They encourage new entrants that produce superior results and value and then remorselessly replace the weaker performers who are consuming wealth. Markets have always operated this way. This is the cold heart of capitalism. But now, as with everything else, that heart is beating faster.

> Corporations, on the other hand, operate on an assumption of continuity and become paralyzed within their own culture as they fail to keep up with changing dynamics of the market. Their struggle for survival often takes the form of blind adherence to outdated success models that only serve to inhibit creativity. And as they grow and become more complex they seek to impose control through rules, systems, and procedures that further stifle and discourage innovation.

Foster and Kaplan conclude that corporations wishing to thrive and not merely survive must undertake a total overhaul of their systems and adopt policies that will allow them to "change at the pace and scale of the market." While corporations have traditionally focused on operations rather than evolution, they must now incorporate the concept of discontinuity into their operating philosophy.

> This would entail a fundamental shift of attitude. It requires asking the right questions as opposed to having the right answers. It means hiring, equipping, and motivating the right employees as opposed to controlling them with the tablet-of-stone rules that were once the building blocks of the company.

In other words, it means letting go of the past in order to grasp the future.

An inspiring example of how innovation and creative thinking can help a company thrive in a truly hostile environment is the recent story of Eric Ryan.

Back in the days of the internet boom, Ryan and his partner Adam Lowry were inspired by the way in which Apple Computer had used ultra-chic design to become leaders in the otherwise dull computing industry. So they went looking for their own dull industry and found an excellent candidate in the category of household cleaning products. It was worth about $18 billion in annual sales but had done nothing new since the 1950s. There was a pitiful level of product differentiation with most of the manufacturers only pushing the germ-killing powers of their brands.

"The household cleaning aisle was so big, yet everything was so boring," Ryan said. Perfect!

Ryan and Lowry entered the market as rank outsiders with very little money. But they had a powerful advantage. They had an idea. They decided to create a brand of household cleaning products that would appeal to the fashion sensibilities of hip, young urbanites.

"Your house is this high-interest, high-emotion place but the products people used for it were just commodities," Ryan said. "We were the first ones to treat cleaning as cool."

With $200,000 borrowed from friends and family, they set about creating a range of products that people would want to display on their shelves. They employed a world famous designer, Karim Rashid, to develop a minimalist style of packaging—a series of very cool-looking soap bottles shaped like teardrops and bowling pins. And they developed an exotic range of scents— cucumber, lavender, and mandarin orange—fragrances that were actually pleasant, as opposed to the hospital-pinewood standard.

The results make a very strong statement about the power of innovation and creative thinking. Most of the dot-coms that were vying to buy up Ryan six years ago are now extinct—dead and buried.

But his company, Method Products, has recently been named the seventh fastest growing privately held company in America by *Inc.* magazine. Its revenue shot from $156,000 in 2002 to $3.4 million in 2003 and, although the company doesn't disclose its figures, Information Resources Inc. estimated its sales at $44.9 million for the year ending August 2006. And that does not include its income from Walmart! *Inc.* magazine estimated that Method's revenues have grown by 3,390% over the last three years.

It's a jaw-dropping tale. And the size of their achievement makes it easy to overlook one very significant fact.

Any of their competitors could have done it.

Clorox, with $4.4 billion in sales, NPD resources and expertise, production facilities, and established distribution channels could easily have created a new brand that appealed to trendy young householders. But they didn't. And nor did any of the other industry giants operating in the category.

Why?

They didn't see the opportunity, because they didn't look for it and then create it. They didn't innovate, they hoped a comfortable past would continue and become their profitable future.

In short, they didn't evolve. Which brings us back to the purpose of this chapter. To establish the fact that innovation and creative thinking are now mandatory competencies if you are going to succeed.

Daniel Pink, in his book, *A Whole New Mind: Why Right-brainers Will Rule the Future*, looks at how the workforce is evolving.

We're moving from a knowledge economy into what he describes as "The Conceptual Age." It's now less about what you know and more about what you can create. Old knowledge is cheap; new knowledge is where the money is going.

But it's not just the corporation's future that is uncertain. Yours is too.

And that future, as we have seen, is happening faster ever day.

If you are going to evolve, to survive and thrive, then you too will need to think more creatively.

And you'll need to do it faster, too.

3. Rediscovering your creativity

At the start of every creative workshop I run, I ask the group this simple question:

"Who here would describe themselves as a creative person?"

The response is consistent and revealing. And yet I always find it surprising.

In a fairly mixed audience, I'd be lucky to see 30% of people raising their hands. Usually, I might see 20% who have the courage to raise a hand fully and a smattering of those who raise their hand to half-mast while looking nervously around to see what level of confidence their colleagues are displaying.

I have noticed that in a predominantly female group I will get a better showing. On occasion I have had 60% or so of the room own up to a belief in their creative talents. (And that is consistent with research into differences between male and female brain development.)

Recently, at a conference of about 140 people from the Sales and Marketing department of a large and extremely successful financial investment company, I saw as few as 14 hands reach hesitantly for the ceiling. That's a dismal 10%. This attitude reveals two significant things. First,

by and large, people have little confidence in the idea that they are creative.

Second, if our economic growth and industries are dependent on innovation and creative thinking to survive and thrive, then we have a problem. It seems only a small percentage of the employees in our workforce genuinely feel they can make a personal contribution to this endeavor.

This further suggests that, in any industry, there will be a minority group that is struggling to create a future for the company while the majority stands back and passes judgment on their plans and initiatives. This can quickly develop into a rift, an adversarial relationship that is very costly in the attrition rate of new ideas. It's an unfortunate fact but, when judging new ideas, most people tend to be negative. They see problems before they see opportunities.

Why do we behave like this? We have, as a community, a strange attitude toward the word "creativity."

Anthony Storr, in his book *The Dynamics of Creation*, points out that the word "creativity" does not appear in the third edition of the *Shorter Oxford English Dictionary*. And yet it is in widespread use—particularly, these days, in the world of business. It has been defined elsewhere as "The ability to bring something new into existence." That is a workable definition for the purposes of this book but it's not consistent with the way society has chosen to define "creative people."

We take a limited and limiting view of the characteristics that are required before one is honored with the title of "creative person."

In terms of creative ability, we have organized ourselves into a pyramid.

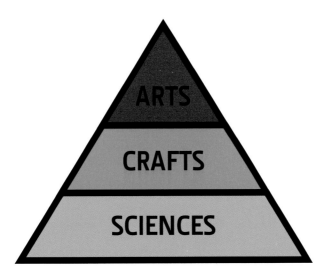

At the top we put the Arts—painters, sculptors, writers, poets, photographers, film directors, actors, performers, and so on. These people constitute a gifted elite in our estimation. They are respected, celebrated, and highly rewarded when successful.

Beneath them we have the Crafts. This group, while displaying many artistic skills, lacks a degree of artistic vision. While their work may be brilliantly executed, there is little chance of the controversy that often surrounds a true artist. In their work, technique and style triumph over intellectual content. (For example, a portrait photographer may be described as an "artist" because of his interpretive style and unusual imagery, whereas a pack-shot photographer in advertising is decidedly a craftsman. Unless or until he does something unusual or bizarre.)

And relegated to the base of this pyramid we find the scientists, engineers, and mathematicians —people whose lives are supposedly a prison of logic and reason. There is something distinctly unglamorous about this group. You are unlikely to see pictures of their homes or read about their extramarital affairs in the magazines at the supermarket checkout.

But just the briefest investigation of this pyramid reveals it to be complete nonsense. It's an unfounded prejudice, but unfortunately, one that affects us all.

It's actually down in the base of the pyramid that we find the inventors, the scientists, mad or otherwise, who through inductive reasoning and chance discovery, actually make sense of the world and enable us to progress. Science is the process of "creating" knowledge. And we underestimate the role that imagination plays in this work.

Art, on the other hand, is frequently plagiaristic and repetitive and yet we reward its practitioners with the highest accolades. (Try watching the Grammy Awards!)

In so doing, society and popular culture have created an absurd pecking order. Arty types at the top, geeky types at the bottom. (Ever wondered about the creative brilliance required to design a software package?)

I'd love to see this pyramid inverted. We need an Academy Awards for such categories as "Best development of a new transplant procedure." We do have the Nobel Prize, but it's hardly prime-time viewing.

Why is this? Why do we marginalize creativity by giving it such a limited definition?

Certainly our education plays a very significant role.

In his book, *Zen and the Art of Motorcycle Maintenance*, Robert Pirsig says little about Buddhism or mechanics but he does introduce a concept he calls the "Classic–Romantic Split."

Most Western education systems force children, during their teenage years, to make a decision. Are they going to follow a career in the Sciences (the Classics) or the Arts (the Romantics)? The two are seen as mutually exclusive. The "streaming" of the curriculum, once this decision has been made, requires a near-total commitment to the chosen area of study. There is no opportunity for a "Renaissance Man" education. It's one or the other.

As we shall see later in this chapter, these children are being asked to decide which hemisphere of their brain is going to provide them with their best future and standard of living—left or right.

So how is this decision made? Quite simply, by hunch. Children who have shown a liking for numbers, chemistry, or biology projects and other process-driven activities, will be advised to follow a career in the sciences. They join the Classics. And those who learned a musical instrument, have an aptitude for languages, or were good at drawing will be told to throw their lot in with the Romantics.

It's left brain versus right brain.

But it is worth remembering that children at this age, 15–19, are at the outset of their voyage of self-discovery. There is nothing fixed in their preferences and abilities. These are yet to be revealed.

And, during these years, their self-esteem is very fragile. If they are told that their drawings are not very good, they'll quickly learn to believe that they are not artistic. They are unlikely to tell themselves that they need to learn the skill and technique of drawing. They are more likely to believe that they are innately incapable of developing that ability.

It's the same with numbers. Show no aptitude by the age of ten and you are likely to hear that you are not good at mathematics. And that implies, or you'll infer, that you won't be able to learn this skill and must therefore learn to work around the limitation.

Most mainstream education confuses preferences with competencies and imagines them to be one and the same. Few systems acknowledge that a preference might change and a new competency can quickly develop.

And so Pirsig believes that the creative die is cast before we even reach university education. We are one or the other—a decision that ignores that fact that creativity is essential, absolutely mandatory, if one is to excel on either side of the Classic–Romantic divide.

Edward de Bono, in his writing on Lateral Thinking, believes our creative potential is crushed at an even earlier age.

He refers to the Three Stages of Childhood—

The What?, The Why?, The Why Not?

We start by identifying the objects we find in the world. "What is this, what is that?" And usually we get the answers.

Then we question the meaning and purpose of things. "Why this, why that?" And we get some answers, some but not all of them satisfactory.

Then we question the rules. "Why not?"

And the answers we receive at this early age are, for most of us, wholly unacceptable. Some family favorites: "Because that's not the way we do it." "Because I say so." "Go ask your mother!" And so on.

De Bono would assert that, at this early age, we are strangling our primary resource for creative thinking—our curiosity. Without it, we'll never ask questions and undercover the hidden potential of things. We'll accept the status quo.

There is a further hindrance to the development of our creative potential. We don't teach it. **We don't learn to think creatively at school**. We don't study and understand techniques for creative thinking. We don't even encourage the belief that it is a skill that can be learned.

Consequently, we see it as a gift. It's innate. You are either born with it or you are born without it. Rather like a sense of humor. If you don't have one, it's hard to develop. No one is likely to show you a technique by which you can better enjoy a good joke or see the funny side of life.

And so this notion of creativity as a gift gives it a rarity value. Which in turn makes those that possess it rather special. Now we can start to see the false edifice of logic that has constructed our "Creative Pyramid."

Here it is: Creativity exists mostly in the domain of the Arts, where only God's chosen few are gifted with this innate ability. Therefore they are an elite. They are, and should be, at the very pinnacle of the pyramid.

I exaggerate to make the point. But this is the underlying view that society takes of creativity.

It's highly pejorative and one that undermines the confidence of those who need to think creatively in areas that are unrelated to the Arts—particularly in the area of business.

And I think it explains some of the reluctance I see in large groups where so few are prepared to raise their hands and, in so doing, claim an apparently superior place in the room. Perhaps modesty, as well as a lack of confidence, prevails.

So how are we to overturn these false beliefs and assumptions?

We can start by returning to our initial definition of creativity, "the ability to bring something new into existence," and remind ourselves that this in no way implies that creative activity is limited to the Arts. Far from it. As we saw in Chapter 1, all organisms, be they ones we find in nature or in the world of commerce and business,

use creativity as their engine of change and evolution.

So what personal competencies must we develop to make a useful contribution to that process?

The most effective tool is one with which we are all born.

Our imagination.

It's the combination of curiosity and imagination that makes all human beings fundamentally creative. We wonder and we speculate about how different the world, our world, could be. And we do this on many different levels.

We become creative when we apply our imagination in such a way that we "bring something new into existence." (And we become innovative when that "something" proves itself to be useful.)

Often, when confronted with a workshop group that has declared itself to be predominantly "uncreative," I'll ask everyone to take a simple test by answering these five questions:

1. Do you ever drive to work and then, after parking your car, realize that you can't remember the journey? You've been on autopilot. You can only hope that had a child chased a ball into the road, you would have suddenly had the presence of mind to jump on the brakes.

2. Do you ever read a page of a book and before you get to the end realize that you haven't absorbed a word? Do you have to go back and read the words as if for the first time?

3. Do you ever prepare for a conversation? Do you write it in your head? You might be about to make a phone call or take someone out on a date and so you mentally prepare some dialog that anticipates not only your own comments but also their likely replies.

4. Do you ever find that, after an argument in which someone got the better of you, you rescript the entire altercation in your mind? Only in this version you are cruelly triumphant. Your opponent becomes a pitiful adversary, horribly skewered on your wit and barbed retorts?

5. Do you ever daydream or indulge in wild fantasies and flights of imagination in which you are a different version of yourself?

The answer to the first four questions is usually an immediate "Yes."

Some people struggle to confess to number 5 but will eventually concede that they spend some of their waking lives in a dreamlike state. (Fantasies are very private affairs conducted within the safe and private confines of our minds. A workshop full of colleagues is no place to be sharing them.)

So where does our mind wander on these occasions?

We escape into our imagination.

In fact, we live in our imagination. The reason we have seen such a proliferation of "Here and Now" philosophies on the self-help bookshelves is that it's so hard to stay here in the present.

Some years ago I was studying Philosophy at the School of Economic Science in London and our tutor set us a simple challenge. He asked us to stay in the moment, to maintain a continuous awareness of our surroundings, for the time it took us to leave the classroom and reach the pavement outside our building.

We all failed. Even those of us who didn't get caught up in a conversation found that our minds soon wandered off into our imagination.

Daydreaming is a voluntary excursion into an unreal world. And it's amazing what we accomplish there.

Try this test now.

Close your eyes for a few minutes and indulge yourself in a particularly vivid daydream. Ensure that it is one you enjoy. Maybe you have a favorite subject. (Recently, a young woman in one of my workshops assured me that "all men fantasize about being rock stars." Few, if any, of the men in the group disagreed with her. I didn't!)

Do this until you feel the dream has run its course and reached some sort of satisfying conclusion. Now, ask yourself a few questions about what was going on.

Did you see other people in the dream?

Did they speak to you or to each other?

Did you see where the dream was taking place? Was the environment or location apparent?

Did the dream have some sort of narrative structure? A beginning, middle, and end? Did it reach a conclusion?

Did you see what people in the dream were wearing or not wearing?

Did you notice any details about people in the dream?

Daydreams, particularly ones in which we deliberately get involved, can be quite cinematic. We watch them on our imagination's internal video display. Let's imagine that you could twist your ear or pinch your nose and a DVD would pop out of a slot in the top of your head. This DVD contains the daydream you have just enjoyed. (We always enjoy our daydreams. Unlike movies, if they get boring we just change and improve them while they run.)

Now, if we were to pop that into a DVD player we could watch your fantasy together. No doubt you'd find the prospect hideously embarrassing while we had a good laugh. But if we could get through the experience, at the end of your short mental film we might come to a title sequence.

It would look something like this.

Director .... **You**
Writer .... **You**
Cinematographer .... **You**
Art Director... **You**
Wardrobe.. **You**
Hair & Make Up .... **You**

And so on.

You get all the credits. You did all the work. The point to make here is that, without any effort at all, you used all of the skills we celebrate so extravagantly every year at the Oscars. And one assumes that you did a good job or you would have changed it yourself without any prompting from either an audience or the critics.

So, even if you are one of those people who make the absurd statement, "I don't have a creative bone in my body," (and there are many who do), then remember

you have an imagination that is probably more powerful than you are

and which you find hard to escape throughout most of the working day.

The question is how do you put it to good use. How do you attach your imagination to a creative purpose?

To better understand that problem we need to take a closer look at what Woody Allen called his "second favorite organ."

The brain.

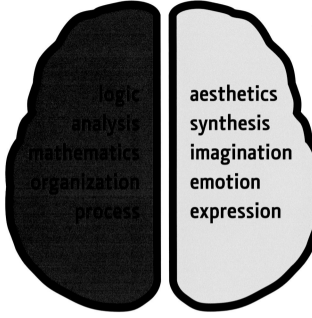

logic
analysis
mathematics
organization
process

aesthetics
synthesis
imagination
emotion
expression

Roger Sperry Brain

Most of us are familiar with the concept of the brain being divided into two halves, left and right, which are connected by a cord called the *corpus callosum*.

Roger Sperry won the Nobel Prize for developing a model that explains the differences in functionality between one side of the brain and the other.

Briefly, his findings suggest that the left side of the brain is our logic center. Here we perform tasks that require analysis, mathematical computation, organization, and the development and use of process. The right side of our brain is where our imagination resides. Here we appreciate aesthetics and music, we synthesize ideas and we feel and express emotion.

One of his most significant observations was that the bilateral organization of the brain reflects and encourages the human inclination to express preferences.

Wherever we find a duality or choice, we develop a preference.

We have a preferred hand for writing, a preferred eye for seeing, a preferred foot for kicking a ball.

What is important to note is that, while we express a preference, we still maintain a competence in both faculties. We can learn to write with our other hand, we can see perfectly well with both eyes, and both legs remain fully operational. In other words, just because you prefer to do one thing doesn't mean you are incapable of doing the other. Preferences and competencies are very different and one does not exclude the other.

Some years later, another Nobel Prize-winning scientist, Paul MacLean, developed a different theory of the way the brain works.

His triune, or three-in-one, concept divides the brain not from left to right but from bottom to top. In MacLean's "Evolutionary" theory, the brain developed from its reptilian form at the top of the spine into a mammalian brain in front of it. Finally, the human brain formed of top of the mammalian brain, just behind our forehead.

Ignoring the reptilian brain, which provides controls for essential bodily functions and autonomic responses, we can interpret MacLean's brain as one with a front and a back. The front is the neo-cortex, which gives us intellect and the ability to think and reflect, and the back is the mammalian, limbic system that contains our feelings.

So how de we reconcile these two apparently correct but strikingly different views of how the brain is built?

There lies the genius of Ned Herrmann. Somewhat unfairly it seems, Herrmann didn't win a Nobel Prize for making sense of what, at first, appear to be two contradictory theories.

His "Eureka" moment came when he decided both were right.

Ned Herrmann was an industrial psychologist working for General Electric who developed a profiling system to understand the preferences and competencies of the company employees. He was an education specialist with a particular interest in creativity.

His concept of the Whole Brain developed when he overlaid Sperry's left brain, right brain concept on top of MacLean's front brain, back brain model.

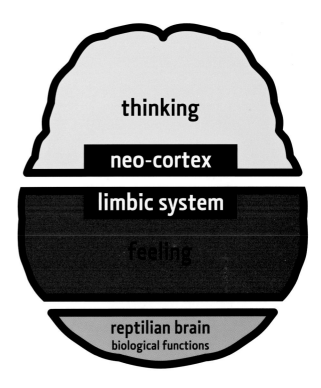

Paul MacLean Brain

The result is the four-quadrant metaphor for the brain's preferences as shown in this diagram.

The beauty of Herrmann's research is that, once again, it stresses that **preferences do not build one competency and in the process destroy another**. So even if you have a preference for the behavior described in the green quadrant, you retain a competency for activity in the yellow. Or to put it simply, to have a love of systems doesn't mean you can't think creatively. That competency remains whether you use it or not.

However, further research has shown us how a preference can blind us to the fact we have a competency.

logic analysis facts numbers	art imagination improvisation synthesizing
planning organization administration attention to detail	emotions expressions talking interpersonal feelings

Ned Herrmann Brain

Take a look at the Necker Cube below. Study it for a minute or so and you'll see that two images of the cube emerge. In one the dot is on the outside and in the other it is on the inside at the back. With little effort we can switch from one optical image to the other.

However, research has shown that if you were rewarded for seeing the dot on the outside, very soon you would find it difficult to see the dot on the inside. This suggests that when we are rewarded for using a preference we become progressively less aware of the competency we have abandoned.

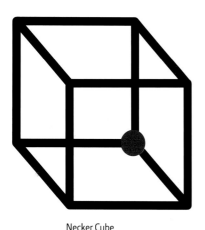

Necker Cube

Think of this in the context of working life. If you have always been rewarded for being a green-quadrant employee who excels at systematic thinking, you will have lost sight of the creative and imaginative competencies that operate in your diametrically opposed yellow quadrant.

Similarly, if you are rewarded for your blue quadrant analytical abilities, you may lose sight of the feelings and interpersonal concerns that would normally be expressed in your red quadrant.

But as we can see from the Necker Cube example, these abilities are still latent within you. **If different behavior is rewarded, both your preferences and therefore your competencies may change.**

I used to see this frequently in advertising agency life. As a Creative Director I would sometimes bring into the creative department people whose career history did not suggest they would excel at conceptual thinking. And yet, they would quickly adapt to the environment and magically become "creative."

What had changed?

Environment, reward, and encouragement.

An understanding of this dynamic is essential if we are going to acknowledge and then develop our potential as creative thinkers.

It's my firm belief that creativity is not a gift, it's a skill which we can learn. In the right environment, with the right processes and tools, and with the right rewards, we develop that skill faster.

There is mounting evidence in research to show that

the brain, like a computer, can be programmed and reprogrammed.

Louis Cozolino, in *The Neuroscience of Psychotherapy*, examines how brain scanning can reveal the way in which new ideas create new thought patterns that cause the brain to change how it physically processes information.

We think by creating dendrite connections in the neural pathways of the brain. Neurologically, this is called "use-dependent plasticity." If we don't continue to create new neural pathways the brain starts to atrophy.

Some years ago a group of psychologists conducted a research project in a nunnery. Within the community they found many nuns who had reached ages of 80 and 90 without showing any signs of senility. The explanation was that they spent their spare time solving riddles and lateral-thinking problems. In this way they maintained the "plasticity" of their minds.

Habit unfortunately causes us to use the same pathways again and again and cause deep grooves in our thinking. In this way we hardwire the brain and start to lose our mental flexibility.

And so the message is clear. Use it or lose it.

If you want to be creative, just start thinking creatively and let the mind start making new connections.

4. The Box: What is it and how do we get out of it?

If you were a fly on the wall in any meeting room where a team has convened to solve a problem, it probably wouldn't be long before you heard this suggestion: "We've got to think outside the box."

What you'd be unlikely to hear is this reply: "What box? What is the box?"

We rarely examine this ubiquitous metaphor for mental paralysis. We don't need to. It perfectly captures the frustration we feel when our imagination is trapped and our thoughts get stuck in a loop. But the "box" metaphor doesn't explain why this is happening to us. And it's only by understanding the walls that confine our thinking that we stand any chance of breaking free and developing new ideas and opportunities.

So let's dismantle the box.

Sometimes it's referred to as the "square," but I prefer the box as it has six sides or walls, and I think there are six common barriers to creative thinking. None of them is impenetrable once you understand how each one has been built.

These walls are Fear, Assumption, Habit, Rules, Knowledge, and Complacency.

Let's take a close look at each one.

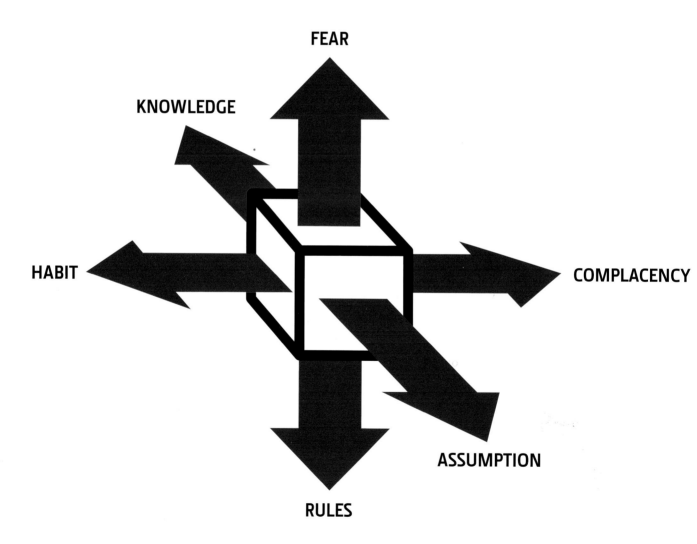

Wall No. 1: Fear

Fear kills creative thinking. It comes in many forms. The most common is probably "fear of the unknown." Creativity always takes us somewhere we have never been before and this may seem dangerous.

> Companies and corporations thrive on predictable outcomes. Those of us who are concerned about shareholders are always aware of this. The stock market is immensely sensitive to targets. Exceeding our estimates is as bad as failing to reach them—it suggests we can't predict our future. Either way we pay a penalty.

In my experience the Holy Grail of business, particularly bigger businesses, is to find an idea that is fresh and new and yet brings the reassurance of having been tried and proven in the past. That's never going to happen.

A new idea always arrives untested, without any guarantees as to how it will develop and perform in the future.

Which is why a fear of the unknown can trigger another very common fear, one that haunts the corridors of many of the companies I have visited over the years.

> A fear of failure.

> Failure is very visible in a commercial environment and the price is usually high. Someone gets fired. This makes us innately cautious. New ideas become a threat first and an opportunity second. That's a climate in which creativity will never thrive as it feeds on optimism, confidence, and commitment.

There is also a more personal fear that can stop our creative juices flowing. And it's one we keep to ourselves. We are afraid of looking foolish.

> Most of us have sat in a brainstorming session and wrestled with our inner critic—that little voice that loves to whisper "garbage" before we spit out an idea and submit it to the scrutiny of the room.

We are very attached to our ideas. They are the children of our minds. We are protective, often over-protective of them. And we identify with them very closely. If our ideas our attacked, denigrated, or rejected, we don't feel sorry for the idea, we feel sorry for ourselves and our injured pride.

This level of **self-consciousness destroys another essential condition for fertile thought. Spontaneity**.

Few things are more frustrating than to think of an idea and then withhold it through fear of ridicule only to see someone else suggest it to unanimous approval and applause. We've all heard someone say, "Yes, I was just thinking that myself." But they didn't say it. And the price for that is that it's now someone else's idea. This climate of fear that surrounds creative thinking can be very destructive.

A colleague of mine has a poster on his wall that warns him against the "Killer Phrases" that destroy ideas before they have a chance to prove themselves.

Here they are:

1. It'll never work
2. We don't have the time
3. It's not in the budget
4. The Boss will never go for it
5. We've always done it this way
6. That sounds stupid
7. Let's see what the committee thinks
8. It's not our style
9. I've seen that before somewhere
10. The last person who suggested that doesn't work here anymore (My personal favorite.)

These should inspire fear in the most reckless employee!

But the fact remains that new ideas are unproven. That doesn't necessarily mean they are dangerous.

Ideas are like electricity. They contain tremendous energy but are only harmful when handled carelessly.

And I genuinely believe there is no such thing as a bad idea until you act on it without due consideration. In fact, bad ideas are frequently the stepping stones to good ideas.

We have a saying at the office:

"The road to brilliance is often paved with absurdity."

It's true. Our minds can operate an alchemical process that takes mad, bad, and apparently dangerous ideas and turns them into gold. (We'll look at some tools for doing this in Chapter 9.)

But, for that to happen, we need to create a "Fear-Free Zone" where we can experiment with new ideas without fear of the consequences. I came across a wonderful example of this in the investment banking category —a business that, for the purpose of reassuring its clients, often downplays its dependence on the uncertainty and unpredictability of creative thinking.

One of the most successful firms in Sydney, Australia, mandates that all of its investment advisors have two portfolios—one real, one imaginary. The firm's clients are in the real portfolio. It's real money that is being invested and, at the end of the year, the returns in this portfolio will decide how the company performance is evaluated by clients and the general public. In the imaginary portfolio there are no real clients and no money is actually changing hands. All investments are hypothetical. But these fake transactions have to be made in line with the market realities. The imaginary portfolio may not actually exist but it performs exactly as if it did.

The genius of this concept is that, at the end of the financial year, the advisor is assessed and rewarded by his employers on the value of his imaginary and not of his real portfolio. He's judged on his ability to perform in a fear-free zone. His creativity is being encouraged and tested.

Of course the management knows that any great ideas that perform well in the imaginary portfolio will be imported into the real portfolio. So the company's real clients are benefiting from the experience of those clients who don't actually exist. This parallel universe accounts for much of the company's success as it creates a space where people can act with confidence.

And **confidence is the only real antidote to fear**.

Few business cultures know how to instill this attitude in their staff. And we'll look at how we might achieve this in Chapter 10.

But at Digital Domain, the special effects production house in Los Angeles, I saw an unusual and probably quite effective way of doing it. Their T-shirts bore this inspiring motto:

"Fear is not an option."

Wall No. 2: Assumptions

I like the old adage that goes, "to assume is to make an **ass** of **u** and **me**." Assumptions are dangerous because they encourage us to think we know more than we do.

Like the lenses in a pair of glasses, assumptions act as filters that change the way we see things.

And like lenses, we don't notice that we are wearing them. And so we believe things are the way we see them and make no allowance for possible distortion.

When we pass our assumptions onto other people as facts and truths, we bend and blur their vision of reality.

It's an insidious process.

To make the point, try solving this simple problem.

A traffic cop is sitting in his patrol car beside the road. He's on duty and looking for driving offenders. Suddenly a woman zooms past him and, without signaling, turns into a one-way street ignoring the sign that clearly shows the traffic is coming toward her. She doesn't slow down. In fact she speeds up and, without signaling, turns into another one-way street, again going against the traffic. The cop does nothing. He sees it all and decides to take no action. Why?

If the answer is not obvious, give this problem a couple of minutes. (Any more would probably be a waste of your time. This type of problem is either solved quickly or not at all.)

Got it? Struggling? If you want the answer, skip to the last page of this chapter and you'll find it at the bottom of page 55.

Now, if you didn't know the problem and then solved it, or gave up and read the solution, you'll have just enjoyed an "Aha!" moment—a moment where you are struck by a sudden realization.

In this case you will realize that your efforts to solve the problem were hampered by the assumption that the woman was in a car. The reason for that is context. Everything about the context of the problem suggested driving. The fact that she didn't use turn signals is perfectly consistent with the fact that joggers don't feel the need to tell us where they are going, preferring to swerve in and around us.

But the fact that the problem mentions turn signals sends your thoughts down a neural pathway that has been grooved by considerations of driving and road safety. This, in part, explains why if you struggled to solve the problem you are unlikely to hit on the answer after two minutes have passed. In that time you have progressed from a neural pathway to a neural highway where there are no U-turns allowed. Once your mind is committed to a particular direction of thought it is hard to make a detour or diversion. Especially as the hidden nature of assumptions means you do not even suspect you have taken a wrong turn.

The only way to escape this problem is to challenge assumptions at the beginning of the journey.

When analyzing a problem, particularly one that requires a new solution, it's essential that we separate what we know from what we assume.

Here's another riddle that gives you an opportunity to practice.

A stranger moves to a new town. He knows no one there and no one knows him. In his first year he finds work and marries a local girl. He decides to stay and settles down. Over the next year he marries two other women but never gets divorced. Bigamy is illegal in this town. Everyone knows what he has done. In fact a local politician acted as a witness at his first wedding and attended the second. He is not prosecuted. He and all three women live openly and fearlessly. How can this happen?

If the answer is not immediately obvious, write a list of every assumption you are making about this scenario. Challenge everything you think you know. If necessary, question any possible ambiguity in the words that describe the situation. (This is a clue!) Often we assume a word means one thing when in fact it can mean something quite different. Still stuck?

The answer is that the stranger is a perfectly respectable minister who "married" the women by performing their marriage services in the local church. (Aha!) So he married them but didn't end up married to them. However, as you may have experienced, once we have pictured him as a husband, it's hard to turn back and create the opportunity to see him as a man of the cloth.

Adjacent to the wall built of assumptions, we find another wall that is also difficult to climb.

Wall No. 3: Knowledge

Knowledge is Assumption's bigger, stronger brother.

They can look alike and are often confused for one another.

And Knowledge has an evil twin, Ignorance. They may be opposed to each other but they remain closely related.

It seems obvious to say that ignorance will hinder our ability to think creatively. Surely, if we don't know the full facts of a situation we can't generate ideas that will provide an appropriate solution.

That may be true but it's not that simple.

The problem with ignorance is the old adage of

You don't know what you don't know.

So how do you know that you don't know it? How do you recognize and understand your ignorance so that you can correct it? Knowledge creates a similar conundrum.

Take a quick look at the two lines below and answer these questions.

Is the top line longer?
Are the lines the same length?
Is the bottom line longer?

A

B

If the groups and workshops I conduct are anything to go by, most of you will have answered that the lines are the same length.

Take a closer look.

The line on the bottom is longer.

Why did you get this wrong when the problem was staring you in the face? Take the arrowheads and tails off the two lines and you would immediately, and without difficulty, see which is longer.

But you didn't look that closely.

What you saw was a problem to which you already knew the answer. You'd seen it before and therefore believed you had the required "knowledge" to give the correct answer. No investigation necessary.

Too much knowledge encourages us to believe we are experts and, to borrow from our assumptions-as-lenses analogy, expertise creates a tunnel vision by encouraging us to believe that we are looking at the problem through a microscope. We think we are close to it and seeing it very clearly but in fact we are missing everything that is around it.

Expertise can give us a narrow and highly selective vision.

You can see this in an experiment that was conducted with a group of magicians. They were shown a trick in which a cardsharp could produce an ace from a shuffled pack every time. They were then asked to agree among themselves how the trick was done.

Drawing upon their expertise, they explained how a well-practiced sleight of hand enabled the magician to control and access the exact position of the ace and then pull it from the deck.

The same trick was shown to a group of children. They suggested that all the cards were aces. He could just turn any of them over. Who do you think was right?

It's a simple example of how knowledge can contain and narrow our thinking.

Picasso put it beautifully when he said, "It took me four years to paint like Raphael but a lifetime to paint like a child." He understood well how knowledge and expertise blind us to seeing the world without refraction.

So, as with assumptions, we need to challenge what we know. And we have to uncover what we don't know. (We need to know what we don't know that we don't know. Hard to say as well as do!)

One approach, and we shall explore it further in Chapter 9, is to deny what we do know.

There was a time when we knew the world was flat. (There are those who still adhere to that belief. Check out The Flat Earth Society website where they claim to have been "deprogramming the masses since 1547").

But Columbus challenged that belief and came up with a great idea: America.

Wall No. 4: The Rules

Rules and Knowledge are quite closely related as rules are predicated on what we "know" or think we "know" to be best for ourselves and for others.

And if what we know is questionable, it follows that the rules must also be open to investigation and challenge.

Particularly as it's not unusual for rules to outlive the conditions in which they were relevant and useful.

Language is a good example.

The rules of grammar and syntax are designed to stop the bastardization of our language. When we talk about the "definition" of a word we are referring to something finite and fixed, as opposed to ambiguous or subject to change. (The British feel quite touchy about this and regard American English as a sloppy and mutated form of their language in which the rules are poorly enforced.)

But language has to evolve as we evolve. As our world changes, so too does the content and the style of our communication—rules or no rules. (Try giving directions to a cab driver in Chaucerian English and see how far that gets you.)

Words, particularly among the young, acquire meanings that are clearly opposed to their original meaning. Think of "wicked" or "sick." But eventually these words are absorbed into mainstream usage. And then the rules bend and dictionaries learn to accommodate these changes. On June 15, 2001, the *Oxford English Dictionary* admitted Homer Simpson's famous catchphrase, "D'oh." On that day it also accepted "Bollywood." (Interestingly, both words are underlined in red and rejected by my word processor, which appears to be lagging six years behind this event.)

In poetry we enjoy a highly creative form of self-expression that thrives on flouting the rules of language. If we subjected modern verse to modern syntax we would destroy its beauty, which is why poetry plays by its own rules.

No one understood this better than T. S. Eliot, who said, "It is not wise to violate the rules until you know how to observe them."

We face much the same predicament in corporate and business life.

Over the years I have worked with several large, multinational companies whose rules have prevented them from adjusting to the changing dynamics of their market.

It's hard for creativity to succeed in such an environment. And it poses a challenge. The old saying "Rules are made to be broken" is a tough call if there is the genuine possibility that it might cost you your job.

Which is why **we need to create a "Rule-Free Zone" as well as a "Fear-Free Zone" in which to experiment**. We need this freedom of thought to prevail, especially when the rules are curtailing and limiting our opportunities. Creativity is a lost cause when an organization starts to suppress new ideas that it fears might challenge the status quo.

I've seen this happen quite recently.

At the completion of a costly campaign development for a multinational advertising client, I was told, "We've got to put this in front of consumers and see what they think." Fair enough, you may say. But these words were from a director who had previously expressed total contempt for the consumer-testing process in the belief that it destroys every shred of creative thinking.

But the rules of his company prevailed. The campaign went into research and quickly ended up in the bin.

Nevertheless, there is one ray of light in this dark picture of repression. Rules, if not always made to be broken, are there to be artfully circumnavigated. Some of our most creative thinking has been inspired by trying to find loopholes in the law.

After all, there was a time when the laws of nature said that man could never fly. Or leave Earth's atmosphere.

Those laws no longer exist.

Wall No. 5: Habit

Habits, rather like assumptions, are insidious. Often, we remain unaware of them until someone else points them out.

> They do serve a useful purpose. They make it easier to get things done—particularly boring things. Many dull tasks can be accomplished by habit while our minds are left free to wander.

Some would even argue that this is a very creative state of mind. Over the years I've heard various people say they get their best ideas when shaving or showering or mowing the lawn. Sadly, it hasn't been my experience.

The problem with habits is that they don't just dull our awareness of what we are doing. They dull our awareness of how we might do it differently or better.

> In this respect they are barriers to creativity. They hinder our progress.
>
> And they are deeply ingrained.

When we drive to work using the same route every day it's because our minds are using the same neural pathway every day. If we took a detour, either physically or mentally, we'd see new and different things. But taking that detour requires a certain presence of mind.

> An entire industry has developed to help people break their habits—smoking, nail biting, procrastinating, losing their temper, to name but a few. It seems that just about any behavior can become habitual to the point of being pathological.

Most techniques for breaking a habit seem to follow a four-stage process: Awareness, Evaluation, Choice, and Substitution. The first step is to become aware of the habit, which is not necessarily as easy as it sounds.

> **In the workplace**, for example, **habits can easily be confused with systems**.
>
> A system is installed to improve the performance of the company and should be subject to periodic review. (Otherwise it becomes a habit.) But a habit develops unconsciously and has to be detected and identified before it can even be considered.

Once that has happened, the second stage is evaluation. All habits have a payoff. Before you can dispense with the behavior it's necessary to understand its value. That way you can understand what will be lost when you dispense with it.

When that is clear you can review and determine your choices. How will you behave differently? What will you get out of it?

And finally, you need to substitute the habit with a more rewarding behavior. Failure to do this almost guarantees that you will end up where you started as you have failed to compensate for the loss of the habit's value.

But even if they are difficult to spot and difficult to change, habits always provide us with a creative opportunity.

Every time you acknowledge a habit, there is the chance to fire up your curiosity and find a creative way of improving what you do.

That is, if you approach it with the right attitude.

Which brings us to the last wall of our box.

Wall No. 6: Complacency

Perhaps the biggest killer of creative thinking is this tired, old attitude: "If it ain't broke, don't fix it."

Complacency sucks the energy, curiosity, commitment, optimism, excitement, desire, and sense of opportunity out of any creative challenge. And it's a virus. Once complacency infects a corporate culture, it becomes difficult for even the most highly motivated people to function well and make a difference. There's no desire to improve because there is a pervasive sense that there is no need to improve. Everything is just fine as it is. Don't rock the boat.

This complacency acts as a thick security blanket for those who are afraid of change. And it's usually an attitude that can be defended with what sounds like common sense.

"We've tried something like that before and it didn't work."

"Right now, it's not worth the time or expense. We have other priorities."

All the usual suspects appear when a complacent culture is faced with someone who feels there is perhaps a better way of doing things.

Unfortunately, this is a senior management issue.

While I was working in Tokyo I heard an expression I loved: **"The fish rots from the head down."** This is very true of the way in which a management team sets the standards and attitudes that become the operating culture of a company.

If management is complacent, it's unlikely that the employees will be able to invigorate their colleagues. Individual departments might take a more creative approach to their assignments and opportunities, but without the full and vociferous support of the senior executives, their efforts will be unsupported and undermined.

The consequences are dire.

In our brief look at the domestic cleaning category we saw how complacency led to stagnation and then vulnerability when a more energetic and creative competitor entered the field.

We see this in all categories and, as we've already noted, size is no protection when a company fails to evolve. Oldsmobile, for example, was an automotive giant throughout much of its history. It's now an automotive dinosaur. Extinct.

So how do we fight complacency? Treat it as a habit.

First identify it. Be aware of it. Make everyone aware of it. Especially the executives.

Second, understand its value. This will turn out to be pitiful. Complacency does no more than make life easier and less stressful in the short term. It masks laziness and a lack of initiative.

Then understand its cost. That's usually a loss of competitive advantage leading to a loss of business. Consider your choices. There aren't many. Keep sinking or start swimming.

And finally, replace this behavior with a better attitude. Avoid anything vague. It needs to be an attitude that can be clearly defined so that it will become a vital part of the company's philosophy.

Probably the best philosophy I've heard was practiced by Leo Burnett, the founder of one of the world's largest advertising agencies. He approached every aspect of his business with what he called "**Constructive Dissatisfaction**." He constantly looked for opportunities to do things better, to use his and his company's creative resources to improve the business.

He rewarded all initiatives that supported his philosophy. And it worked. With him at the helm, the company continued to grow throughout his working lifetime.

Constructive Dissatisfaction is a battering ram that can break through all six walls of the box. And there is one aspect of this metaphor that's always worth remembering:

Our mind is not in the box. The box is in our mind.

We made it. Our fears, assumptions, knowledge, rules, habits, and complacency built this little prison. And anything we build, we can dismantle and pull down.

All we need is a process and the right tools.

5. Creative Process! What Creative Process?

I often hear the phrase "creative process" and wonder if there is any such thing. It sounds like an oxymoron.

The value of a process is that it leads to a predictable outcome. But creativity is unpredictable and elusive. It seems to thrive on random thoughts and events and gives us new and unexpected outcomes.

So can we control it and use creative thinking as a practical, problem-solving tool? Yes and no.

There are two types of problems and we don't need creative thinking for both of them. I'm going to call them brainsqueezers and brainteasers. The best way to understand the difference is to solve a few examples of each. To do that, we'll use a series of simple riddles to put your mind through its paces.

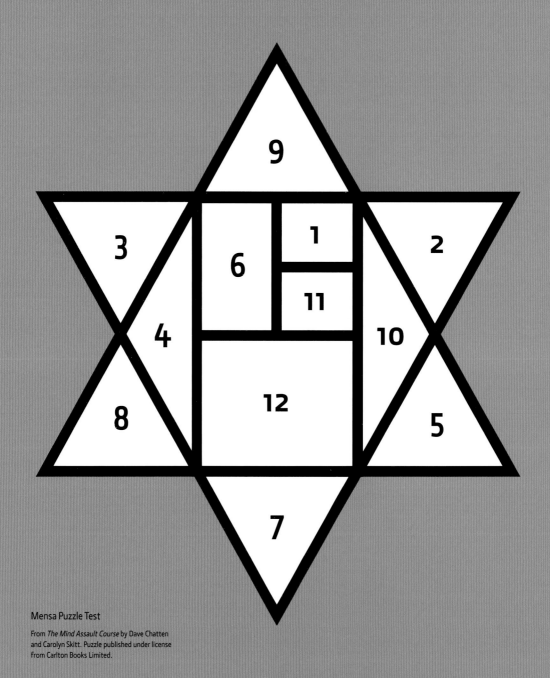

Mensa Puzzle Test

From *The Mind Assault Course* by Dave Chatten
and Carolyn Skitt. Puzzle published under license
from Carlton Books Limited.

Let's start with some Brainsqueezers.

Brainsqueezer No. 1

This is a Mensa puzzle test. Look at the diagram opposite and answer these questions.

1. **How many triangles are there in the diagram?**
2. **How many rectangles are there in the diagram?**
3. **How many hexagons are there in the diagram?**
4. **Deduct the sum of the numbers in the rectangles from the sum of the numbers in the triangles**

Brainsqueezer No. 2

Jones, Brown and Smith all work at the local bank. One of them is the teller, one of them is the cashier and one of them is the manager. The problem is to work out who is in which position.

The only information you have is that the teller was an only child and earns the least of the three.

And Smith, who married Brown's sister, earns more than the manager. So who does what?

Brainsqueezer No. 3

Find a common three letter word knowing the following.

L, A, G, have no common letter with it.
D, R, G, has one common letter but in the wrong place
S, I, D, has one common letter in the correct place
S, I, B, has one common letter in the wrong place
E, I, L, has one common letter in the wrong place

Don't read on until you have either solved the three problems or, at least, worked out the process by which they can be solved. Then check to see if you are right by looking at the bottom of page 67.

Now let's take a close look at how your mind was working.

In the Mensa puzzle the process is simple. You just count. The key is persistence bolstered by the assumption that, as it is a puzzle, there are probably a few hidden shapes. This will encourage you to keep looking beyond the obvious. But the process remains the same. You just have to keep squeezing your brain.

In the case of the Bank you probably homed in on the fact that Brown had a sister and therefore was not an only child and could not be the Teller. That's perhaps the most obvious starting point in the chain of logical deductions that eventually takes you to the answer. As with the Mensa puzzle, you need to be persistent and pursue that logical path to its conclusion.

And it's a similar process with the last one. Logic dictates what is possible and what is not as we move from one line of the puzzle to the next. This, to use Edward de Bono's phrase, is a classic example of "Vertical thinking." Each piece of information supports the information that follows.

With brainsqueezers we always start by searching for information that reveals the underlying logic of the problem.

And once we have found it, we know that we are on our way toward the answer. The path feels like a straight line, and although we might inadvertently take a few detours or stumble now and then, we remain confident that we are on the right track. We just have to keep going.

And when we get to the end of the process, we feel relieved. The effort is over. We can stop squeezing and relax. We also feel reasonably confident that our answer is right, but perhaps not 100% sure. Sometimes there may be a lingering uncertainty. We only feel truly relieved when our solution is confirmed to be correct.

Now let's try some brainteasers. There are many books of these problems on the market and I've included five in the hope you won't have seen at least one or two of them before.

Brainteaser No. 1

A man goes into a hardware store on a Monday to buy some items. He buys seventeen and pays $14. The next day another man goes in and buys six and pays $7. On the following Thursday a man goes in and buys 103 and only pays $21. They are all buying the same things and the price per item has not changed. How can this be true?

Brainteaser No. 2

A retired British General from the Second World War is walking in London when he sees an elderly beggar with a sign that reads, "War veteran." He gives the man some money but snatches it back when the beggar thanks him. Why?

Brainteaser No. 3

In Britain, how was an archaeologist able to ascertain that the occupying Roman forces had always driven their chariots on the left side of the road?

Brainteaser No. 4

A father and his son are driving in their car and have an accident. The father is killed immediately but the son, badly injured, is taken by ambulance to the hospital and prepared for emergency surgery. The surgeon comes into the operating theater and says, "I can't operate on him, he is my son." The surgeon is telling the truth. How can this be so?

Brainteaser No. 5

There are ten flies on the table in front of me. I manage to kill three of them with a single swat. How many are left?

Do these five problems feel very different to the first three?

With a brainteaser there is no obvious point of entry into the underlying logic of the problem. There is no apparent path for our mind to take unless it's a path that leads directly to an answer we think is wrong—as in the case of problem No. 5. Of course there are only seven flies left! But it feels too obvious. It must be a trick. And yet some people stay caught up in the mathematics of the riddle rather than look outside of the numbers and visualize what is actually happening on the tabletop.

Frequently, when confronted with a problem that has no obvious chain of logic, we go blank and our thoughts start to circle round and around. You may have had this experience with the Roman chariots in No. 3. Where do you start? The problem is too vast. There are no clues.

Or we might become fixated on a possibility that never develops into an answer. With problem No. 4 it's common to see people get stuck on the idea that the surgeon is a "religious" father, a father-in-law or some other type of father figure. They might exhaust all variations on that theme while "mother" never occurs to them.

And then there are occasions when we can't sort out helpful information from unhelpful facts and get confused. In problem No. 1, the days of the week are irrelevant but it's impossible to know that. Until you know the answer.

But the big difference between Brainsqueezers and Brainteasers is that

sometimes, when we are trying to solve a brainteaser, the answer just pops into our head.

It comes out of nowhere. The thought process is so fast we can barely remember it. It's just a blur.

We call this an "Aha!" moment.

And after an "Aha!" moment we know we have found the right answer. We are 100% sure. And we don't just feel relieved, we feel surprised. The solution seems so absurdly obvious that we wonder why we didn't see it immediately.

In fact the whole problem looks different. It looks simple and easy.

This never happens with brainsqueezers. With those problems you sense that the information you need is right there in the problem. You just need the dogged determination and brainpower to process it.

But with a brainteaser some element is missing. And it must be provided by your imagination.

With a brainsqueezer you make small, certain steps in a straight line toward the solution. But with a Brainteaser you must make a leap into the unknown and see if you land in the right place. And if you don't, then you must leap again.

This is the difference between inductive and deductive reasoning. One feels predictable and requires the power of reason and logic. The other feels unpredictable and requires the power of imagination.

One says, "Because I know this, it follows I can know that."

The other says, "I don't know that but what if…."

One is logical. One is creative. So here is the big question.

Can we develop a process to solve those problems that don't yield to the process of logic? Can we develop a process that harnesses our imagination so that we can make a leap into the unknown and feel comfortable that we are going to land somewhere near an "Aha!" moment?

Once again, yes and no.

As far as I know, **there is no process that can take us directly to the solution of a creative problem.**

But there are processes that can take us closer to it.

To understand that, let's investigate some moments of inspiration. Perhaps with the benefit of 20/20 hindsight, we can see how it's done. Maybe there is a system.

Galileo, a prolific inventor, had some wonderful "Aha!" moments.

One of them ultimately led to the invention of the clock. He had been pondering the notion of time and wondering how to create a standard measure. He hadn't found a solution. And then one day, in the Cathedral at Pisa, he noticed a priest swinging the thurible, or incense burner, and— "Aha!"—the concept of a pendulum popped into his mind.

Later, he verified his idea by measuring the movement of a pendulum while he timed it against the beat of his heart and observed that it was length and not weight that dictated its speed.

What a stroke of luck that he went to church that day.

Similarly, Isaac Newton was reading a book beneath an apple tree. Newton had been pondering the force that keeps us glued to the planet for some time. But the idea of gravity appeared in a flash as he saw the apple fall. "Aha!"

As with Galileo, he seems to have been in the right place at the right time.

Leonardo da Vinci, in 1490, many years before the Wright brothers took off, invented the helicopter. How? He noticed a carpenter's screw and— "Aha!"—he conceived the notion that a rotary blade could support a plane's weight by screwing it into the sky.

Unfortunately, he didn't have the opportunity to work with the Dutch-Swiss scientist, Daniel Bernoulli, who studied the principles of fluid in motion. His moment came as he was watching a leaf float on water. He noticed that the leaf moved faster as it passed through a constricted part of the stream. "Aha!" Ultimately this led to his development of the Venturi Effect which gave rise to our understanding of how the different pressures above and below an airfoil allow a wing to support a plane in flight.

There's a trend starting to emerge in how these "Aha!" moments occur.

Printed type dates back to 1041 in China. But the printing press was not invented for nearly another 400 years. It might have been longer if Johannes Gutenberg hadn't visited a winery. He'd been struggling with the problem of transferring ink to paper when he watched one of the vintners operate a wine press. "Aha!" The printing press.

James Watt in 1765 was trying to improve upon Newcomen's concept of a steam engine when he watched a kettle boil. "Aha!" We have that moment to thank for the invention of the condenser that eventually led to the steam train.

Archimedes, struggling to calculate the mass of gold in an ornate crown, sits in a bath and notices the water slopping over the edge. "Aha!" The Displacement of Water theory is conceived.

In all these cases, you get the feeling that the creative process was triggered by a random act of luck—the incense burner, the apple, the screw, the leaf, the winepress, the kettle, the bath water.

The trend continues throughout history.

In 1948 George de Mestral was walking in the Jura Mountains when a burr attached itself to his trousers. "Aha!" Velcro.

In the 1890s, the Lumière Brothers struggled to devise a way of projecting film images using a light. They found their "Aha!" by looking at a sewing machine.

In 1940 Helen Barnett Diserens, who worked for the Mum deodorant production team, was impressed by a newfangled invention of the day—the ball-point pen. "Aha!" The roll-on deodorant.

The emerging pattern seems to depend on unpredictable events.

If we try and reduce it to a process it looks something like this:

Step 1. Contemplation

In this phase we think about the problem and learn as much as we can. We try to absorb and understand.

Step 2. Frustration

We get stuck. We have all the available information but something is still missing. We can't move forward and resolve the problem. And, to make the frustration worse, there is no way of knowing how long this phase might last.

Step 3. The Trigger

A seemingly unrelated event affects our thinking. Our mind takes what we're going to call a "Synaptic Swerve" and heads off in a new and unexpected direction. It's this moment that Arthur Koestler, in his classic study of creativity, *The Act of Creation*, describes as the "intersection of two matrices of thought."

Step 4. The Flash

We experience a cerebral spark that clearly illuminates the answer that has been eluding us. It surprises us and is immediately recognizable as being correct.

Step 5. Revelation

This flash of inspiration reveals the problem in an entirely new light. We see it, as if for the first time, and as we will always see it hereafter. The solution, though hard to find, now seems obvious. The problem appears to have been simple.

At this point, it's worth repeating that **this five-point process is only seen with the wisdom of hindsight. It's only obvious when we look back at it**.

So can this system work for us at the start of the ideation process?

Step 1 is not difficult. We study the problem.

Step 2, getting stuck, is unfortunately very easy and comes quite naturally to most of us.

Step 3 is the sticking point. In the examples of breakthrough creative thinking we have just examined, the Trigger seemed to be a random and unpredictable event. And yet, it proved to be extremely relevant.

How can we provoke an unpredictable event that has a relevance we cannot yet imagine? It seems that if we could do that, we could be assured of the Flash that will light up our thinking and reveal the solution to our problem. But if we can't engineer the trigger we remain helplessly dependent on two elements: Time and Luck.

Usually, when solving creative problems at work, time is short. We're working under pressure. That pressure is going to build if we feel we are at the mercy of good fortune. Luck is fickle and there is no reason to believe that it will show up when we need it most.

But like it or not, luck does play a role in creative thinking.

Artists, and particularly poets, have always acknowledged this phenomenon and have a word for it: aleatory. It derives from a Greek word that means "rolling dice."

In the world of business and commerce we tend to shy away from any practice that leaves too much to chance. We seek the comfort of certainty.

But the question remains, can we make our own luck when trying to generate new ideas and solutions to our problems?

Samuel Goldwyn, among others, is often credited with this quote:

"The harder I work, the luckier I get."

Benjamin Franklin said:

"Diligence is the mother of good luck."

And Louis Pasteur, himself a great inventor, made this observation:

"Did you ever observe to whom the accidents happen? Chance favors only the prepared mind."

Their reasoning suggests that there is no escaping Step 1 of the process. We must totally absorb ourselves in everything we know about the problem. That is the diligence, the hard work and the preparation to which they refer.

Triggers may be mere happenstance but it's the way in which we prepare our mind that enables us to notice them. And with the right state of mind and preparedness, we may be able to see Triggers in many unrelated events.

Would Archimedes have discovered the Displacement of Water if he had been washing a cup in a bowl that was too full? Might Newton have been inspired to understand gravity if he had dropped the book he was reading? Or if a bird had crapped on his head? Could Da Vinci have enjoyed an "Aha!" moment and designed the rotary blade after seeing a sycamore leaf twirling in the wind?

Which is more important, the Trigger or the attitude of mind that enables you to notice its relevance and respond to it? In this sense, developing our understanding is how we encourage our own luck. Being completely absorbed in the problem multiplies the number of possible triggers we are capable of seeing. That doesn't mean we can't also manufacture Triggers. We can.

There's one area of life where we do this as a matter of routine. Telling jokes. The punchline of a joke is a Trigger that causes a Synaptic Swerve in our thinking, a Flash of understanding and then reveals a new dimension to the story we have been telling.

The following joke, recently voted the most popular among a poll of comedians, is a good illustration.

Holmes and Watson are lying on the ground and staring up at the stars on a clear summer evening.

"Watson, what do you see?" asks Holmes.

And Watson replies:

"Holmes, I see the majesty of the Lord's creation writ large on the night-time sky. I see the Universe in its vast, mysterious, and unending glory. I see the stars and wonder if, among their infinite number, there is a place where two such individuals as ourselves are now looking down and pondering the same existential conundrum."

"That is very profound Watson."

A moment or two passes in silence.

"And you Holmes. What do you see?" Watson finally asks.

And Holmes' terse reply:

"Watson, I see someone has stolen our damn tent!"

The punch line, in an instant, triggers a Synaptic Swerve that reveals an entirely new understanding of the situation. Gone is the image of two friends quietly contemplating the meaning of Life. It's replaced by the harsh reality of them lying among their possessions after their tent has been stolen while they sleep.

Humor and creativity are closely related. In a joke, the trigger or punchline is only effective if our understanding of the situation has been carefully managed during the setup.

In creative problem solving, the trigger is only effective if our preparation has given us a sensitivity that enables us to notice it.

And so we are going to pursue two strategies.

The first is to prepare the mind.

The second is to make triggers happen.

ANSWERS TO PROBLEMS BRAINSQUEEZERS 1. 14, 7, 2, 18. 2. Brown is the manager, Jones is the teller, Smith is the cashier. 3. **BED. BRAINTEASERS** 1. Numbers for his front door. 2. He says "Danke Schön." 3. He visited a quarry. The tracks were deeper on the left side of the road after the chariots had been loaded. 4. She was his mother. 5. None. The other flies flew away immediately.

6. What's the problem? The real problem?

In our culture, the word "problem" is negative. Problems are seen as the cause of trouble and difficulty. Problems signify a failure of some sort. Problems can be threatening. Therefore, it follows, problems should be avoided.

In Japan, where I lived for four years, problems are regarded as "Golden Eggs." It's good luck to find one. It is a chance to improve something.

This positive context is highly motivating. It moves us from a defensive and fearful attitude to an optimistic and proactive one. Perhaps we need a new word—a hybrid, such as "probbortunity." Kanji, the Japanese formal writing, has one in its depiction of the word "crisis." The hexagram is a combination of "danger" and "opportunity."

Certainly, we need to change our attitude if we are going to change our behavior.

Normally, when faced with a problem, our first instinct is to go looking for a solution. (The sooner we solve it the better!) And if the answer, or the route to the answer, is not immediately apparent, we get frustrated or confused and wonder where and how to make a start. I think this bewilderment comes from the way we were taught at school. In those formative years, we tended to learn both the problems and the answers, and our examination system was, for the most part, a memory test to see if we could recall them accurately and in detail.

However, creative problem-solving requires an entirely different process—one where we must learn to forge our own path from problem to solution. It's less reliant on memory and more on logic, reasoning, and imagination.

Fortunately, there are some principles we can follow. The first of these should be written in stone. It is this:

Start with the problem. Don't go looking for a solution. Look harder at the problem.

Usually, that is where the solution is hiding. That is why, when we finally solve it, we often kick ourselves for having taken so long. And wonder why it took us so long. As we saw in Chapter 5, creative problems often seem simple and obvious in retrospect. The "Aha!" moment is sometimes a gasp of surprise when we realize that the solution has been hiding right under our nose the whole time.

So we must learn to search the problem. We need to dismantle it, view it from every angle, and challenge any assumptions we are making about it. We need to state and restate the problem and, above all, verify it is the right problem and not merely the symptoms of an altogether different one.

The closer we get to the core of the problem, the closer we are to the solution. Charles F. Kettering, the electrical engineer and inventor, summed this up very succinctly when he said:

"A problem well stated is a problem half solved."

This is where the left side of the brain can really do some useful, preparatory work before we engage the right side to do some imaginative and speculative thinking.

In a sense, this is the easy part because it is process-driven.

I'm going to break it down into ten exercises, each of which could form the basis of a workshop module.

1. **Understanding Your Ambitions**
2. **Restating and Reframing the Problem**
3. **Finding the Problems Behind the Problem**
4. **Separating Cause, Problem, and Effect**
5. **Changing Your Perspective**
6. **Identifying the Motivators**
7. **Challenging Your Assumptions**
8. **Extending Your Sphere of Influence**
9. **Overcoming Barriers**
10. **Clarification and Commitment**

Throughout this exercise I'm going to refer to a very simple problem which I first came across in Robert Cialdini's writings on the subject of influence.

It's a true story and we'll use this as a bench test for the work we're going to do.

Here it is:

A 24-hour convenience store is losing customers in the evenings because its parking lot has become the meeting place for local kids. They come to hang out, smoke cigarettes, eat, drink, skateboard, and sometimes to cause trouble—some thefts and damage to cars have occurred. They are not breaking any law by simply being there, but they are making the customers nervous. What can the owners of the store do?

Module No. 1: Understanding Your Ambitions

To borrow a phrase from Steven Covey, we need to "start with the End in mind." We need to think within the context of a positive outcome. This will give a sense of direction to our thoughts but it's not intended to preempt a solution or, in any way, limit our thinking.

Many companies use SMART criteria for assessing outcomes—Specific, Measurable, Attainable, Realistic, Timely.

Similarly, the "What, Why, Who, When" matrix on this page provides a framework of questions that enable you to better understand what you are hoping to achieve. It starts to map out the scope of the problem while retaining the notion of a "probbortunity." It will also start to suggest what roles must be played and within what timeframe a solution must be reached. It's a reality check before any ideation begins.

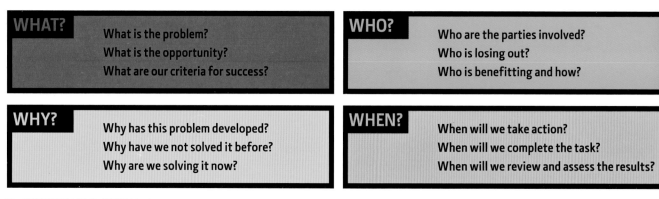

WHAT?
What is the problem?
What is the opportunity?
What are our criteria for success?

WHO?
Who are the parties involved?
Who is losing out?
Who is benefitting and how?

WHY?
Why has this problem developed?
Why have we not solved it before?
Why are we solving it now?

WHEN?
When will we take action?
When will we complete the task?
When will we review and assess the results?

The WHAT, WHY, WHO, WHEN Matrix
Printable version on CD-ROM

Read through these questions with the eyes of the convenience store proprietor and you will see how the issue starts to appear in four dimensions.

One practical virtue of this approach is that it acts as a very good bonding exercise for the team who are going to do the work. It creates a shared understanding, an alignment of ambitions and values, promotes commitment to the task, and is realistic about time and resources needed.

Once that has been done, we can dig a little deeper.

Module No. 2: Restating and Reframing the Problem

Language has a critical effect on how we view the world. We think in words. And words act as on-ramps, stop lights, and intersections on the neural pathways in our minds. Words can and do change the direction our thoughts are taking.

And words mean different things to different people.

Ask anyone what they associate with the word "Life" and you'll get as many answers as people you ask. The word opens up an infinite number of pathways.

But if we follow the discipline of stating and restating the problem ten times, we can get past some of the ambiguities of language and reach a deeper and shared understanding of the issues involved.

Take a look at this simple Restating and Reframing Format.

Write the current expression of the problem in the box at the top.

Now fill out all of the ten alternatives beneath it. Restate the problem ten times, trying to see it from different angles and express it in different words.

Then review the results and compare with the words in the original box.

Do you feel you have moved any closer to the essence or core of the problem you need to solve?

Choose the three most thought-provoking expressions of the problem before you move on. We call these the "Perceived Problems."

Restating and Reframing Format
Printable version on CD-ROM

THE PROBLEM

. . . .

1 . . . .

2 . . . .

3 . . . .

4 . . . .

5 . . . .

6 . . . .

7 . . . .

8 . . . .

9 . . . .

10 . . . .

Module No. 3: Finding the Problems Behind the Problem

Usually, problems don't just appear. They develop. In this module we trace the genealogy of a Perceived Problem to ensure that we are dealing with the root cause and not just the symptoms.

Problems and symptoms are frequently confused and, as we see all too often in medicine, a treated symptom can recur. But a treated problem will be unlikely to re-present symptoms.

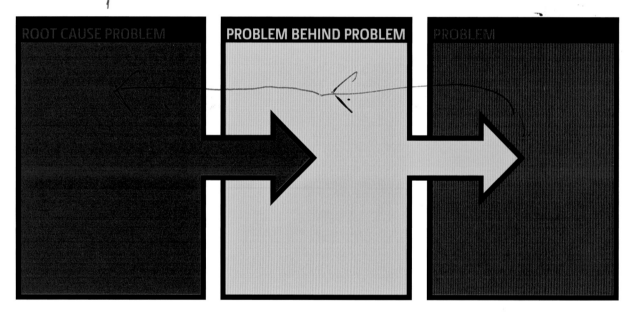

Problem Root Diagram
Printable version on CD-ROM

Write a Perceived Problem in the box on the far right. Then, work against the flow of the arrows. Move to the adjacent box on the left and list any problems that have contributed to the one you are trying to solve.

Start by simply asking this question: "What problems or issues have created my Perceived Problem?"

For example, in the case of the convenience store, you might suggest that lack of parental control or the absence of places for kids to congregate are problems that contribute to what's happening in the parking lot.

Write those in.

And then move one box to the left and repeat the process. See if you can find the factors that contributed to the origin of the Perceived Problem.

> With some problems you'll find a string or chain of causal relationships and with others you may struggle to move more than one box upstream. That doesn't matter. Either is acceptable. The purpose of this exercise is not to fill the flowchart but to reassure yourself that you have worked your way back as far as you can to the causes of the Perceived Problem.

Then, reconsider which problem you need to solve.

> In the case of the convenience store, should we be looking at the problem of customers feeling uncomfortable or intimidated or should we be looking at the problem of the kids having nowhere else to go? This decision will lead to radically different solutions and outcomes. And, on occasion, it will lead you to substitute your Perceived Problem with one that appears to be closer to the source of the issues that created it.

Usually the Perceived Problem will sit in the middle of a continuum that leads from causal factors to consequences. There are likely to be problems that are precipitating the Perceived Problem. And there will be symptoms that we discover to be unacceptable consequences.

> It looks something like this:

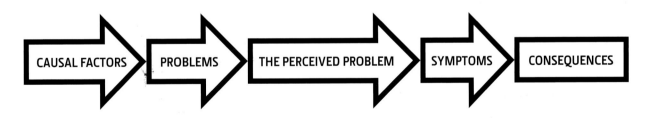

CAUSAL FACTORS → PROBLEMS → THE PERCEIVED PROBLEM → SYMPTOMS → CONSEQUENCES

> Now that we've tried to move upstream and understand the causal factors, let's go with the flow and consider the possible consequences.

Module No. 4: Cause, Problem, Effect

In this module we ask ourselves what will happen if we allow the problem to persist. What if we do nothing? Where will that take us?

The underlying value of this exercise is that it attacks any lingering complacency that has enabled the problem to remain unsolved by showing how it might develop.

Also, while establishing a clear relationship between causal factors, the problem, and its consequences, it continues to help differentiate one from another.

The Cause, Problem, Effect diagram visualizes the causal factors as roots and asks you to decide how these will feed the problem and help it grow and spread from symptoms to eventual consequences.

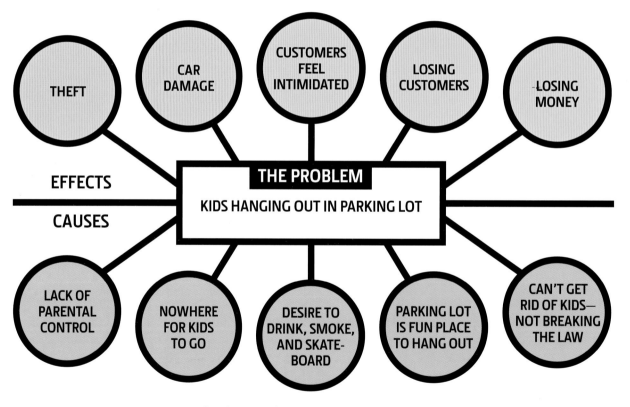

Cause, Problem, Effect Diagram
Printable version on CD-ROM

In this diagram, I've looked at how the problem at the convenience store might grow if action is not taken.

You may disagree and see other ways in which the situation might develop.

Module No. 5: Changing your perspective

If we fail to see a problem as an opportunity, we're more likely to see it as a threat. And when under attack we tend to lose perspective. We become defensive and this narrows our vision.

We can reopen some neural pathways by taking a fly's eye view of the situation.

In this process we start by listing all of the people who are involved. In the case of the convenience store that might be:

**The owners
(the role we are playing)
Our staff
Our customers
The local residents
The kids
The police
The kids' parents**

Then we put the Perceived Problem in the central circle.

Now we take a 360-degree tour around that circle and ask ourselves how this problem would be stated by all of the people who are involved. How would they see it? Or would they see it at all? What might be a problem to you is perhaps no problem at all to other people who are in involved in it.

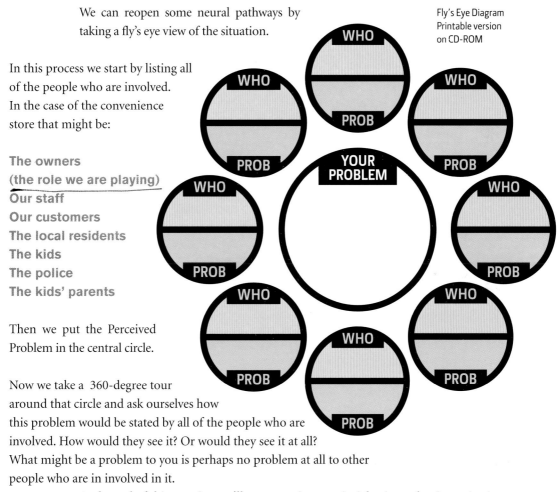

Fly's Eye Diagram
Printable version
on CD-ROM

At the end of this exercise you'll start to gain some insights into what is motivating the people who have allowed this problem to occur and persist. You'll also have a clearer view of who is going to help you and who might oppose you in solving it and creating an opportunity to improve the situation.

Module No. 6: Identifying the Motivators

Whenever human behavior is involved in the creation or the perpetuation of a problem, then someone, somewhere is benefitting. The energy that sustains the situation is coming from this payoff. That means changing the situation will involve someone losing out or making a sacrifice. We need to understand who is winning and who is losing.

This simple process is based partly on what we learn from Maslow's hierarchy of needs and also from what we have observed as the core motivators in business life.

First identify the people who are contributing to the cause of the Perceived Problem. List them in the first column of the Five Whys Format opposite. In the second column, briefly describe their behavior. Then ask the question "Why?" If necessary, ask it up to five times.

NEED
FOR SELF-
ACTUALIZATION

NEED TO KNOW,
EXPLORE, UNDERSTAND

NEED TO ACHIEVE
AND BE RECOGNIZED

NEED TO BELONG, TO LOVE
AND BE LOVED

NEED TO BE SAFE, SECURE,
AND OUT OF DANGER

NEED TO SATISFY HUNGER, THIRST, SLEEP

Maslow's Hierarchy of Needs

Using our example from the convenience store:

Use the Five Whys Format to look at the behavior of the kids and drill down into some of their motivations.

Maslow's pyramid suggests that there are four categories of need—the physical, the emotional, the aesthetic, and the self-fulfilling.

By repeatedly asking the question "Why?" we can establish which of these needs is being met and therefore provides the motivation for the behavior.

In business life we have reduced this hierarchy of needs to a set of just six. They are:

The need to feel secure.
The need to save time.
The need to look good.
The need to make money.
The need to save money.
The need to feel good.

Keep asking the question "Why?" until you have reached the core motivator that explains the behavior.

In doing this, the Five Whys Format will help you establish who is doing what and why. This will provide a useful insight into how your solution to the problem may be met with resistance from those who fear a personal loss or sacrifice. This creates the opportunity for you to find a different way to reward and motivate them within the changes you will propose to make.

WHO?	WHAT?	WHY?	WHY?	WHY?	WHY?	WHY?

The Five Whys Format
Printable version on CD-ROM

Module No. 7: Challenging Your Assumptions

As we saw in Chapter 4, "The Box," assumptions are near-invisible barriers to creative thinking and problem solving. We need to make clear distinctions between what we know, what we think we know, and what we need to know.

This is a very simple left-to-right process.

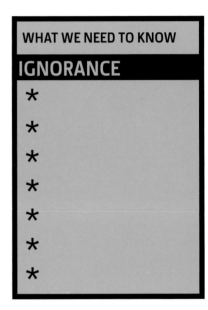

The Assumptions Matrix
Printable version on CD-ROM

In the first column, list the Facts—the truth, the whole truth, and nothing but the truth. What you say must be verifiable.

Or else it belongs in the second column, Assumptions. This is what you think you know; it may be true but, as yet, is unverified or unverifiable.

This process may help you overcome the problem of "You don't know what you don't know." If, in filling in the first two columns, you discover areas of ignorance that might be relevant, put them in column three, the need-to-know column.

Module No. 8: Extending Your Sphere of Influence

This model will help you establish where you should be focusing your efforts.

List all of the people or groups of people who are involved and then plot them on the Influence Diagram below.

In the inner circle put the names of those people or departments you can either directly influence or control. In the next circle, put the names of those who are beyond your control but perhaps still within reach of your influence. In the outer circle, put those who appear to be beyond both your control and your influence.

Then examine the motivators of this outer group (these will be clearly established if you have completed Module No. 6) and ask how you can affect their needs and rewards. This might help you understand how you can move these people into the inner circle of your influence.

It's only then that you will be able to recruit them to support your proposed changes and solution.

Influence Diagram
Printable version on CD-ROM

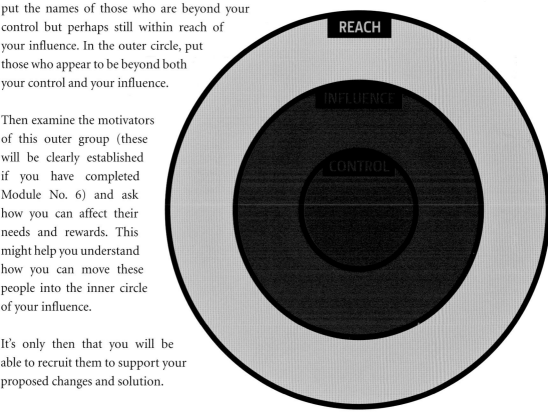

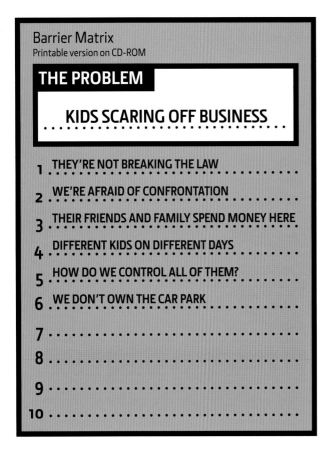

Barrier Matrix
Printable version on CD-ROM

THE PROBLEM

KIDS SCARING OFF BUSINESS

1 THEY'RE NOT BREAKING THE LAW

2 WE'RE AFRAID OF CONFRONTATION

3 THEIR FRIENDS AND FAMILY SPEND MONEY HERE

4 DIFFERENT KIDS ON DIFFERENT DAYS

5 HOW DO WE CONTROL ALL OF THEM?

6 WE DON'T OWN THE CAR PARK

7

8

9

10

Module No. 9: Overcoming Barriers

This module is based on two simple questions.

The first is: "What has stopped us solving this problem?"

All that is required is a list. Again, it's a good bonding exercise for the team as it is exploratory and might reveal some unacknowledged areas of responsibility and influence.

Write the Perceived Problem in the top box.

Then, underneath, list ten barriers that have stopped you solving the problem in the past.

The Barrier Matrix looks at how the convenience store proprietors might have felt they were prevented from taking action.

Then ask a second question of each barrier: "How can we get around it?"

And list those opportunities at the bottom of the page.

Module No. 10: Clarification and Commitment

If you work through most, or at least some of these modules, you should develop a three-dimensional understanding of the problems and opportunities. (Four-dimensional if you agree on a timeframe!)

This puts you in a position to clarify the problem. It's no longer the Perceived Problem; it is the Defined Problem. The team can now make a real commitment to solving it. You're ready to start thinking creatively.

But before we get to that, we should take a look at what really happened at the convenience store.

> I don't know the thought processes of the team that solved this problem. Or even if it was a team, it might have been just one person. So what I'm going to say is purely hypothetical, based on assumption and hindsight, and serves as no more than an illustration of the process we have been exploring.

The ambition of the proprietors was to get the kids to go and hang out somewhere else. They wanted to be free of them.

> The Defined Problem might have been: Kids are loitering in the parking lot, getting up to no good and frightening off our customers.

Behind that problem would be the simple fact that, in the evenings, there was nowhere else to go that was well-lit, where they could skateboard, buy snacks and drinks, and so on.

> We can identify or guess at many causes of the kids' dislocation but the consequences remain the same as far as the proprietors are concerned, i.e. loss of business.

> By changing perspective we can see that, from the kids' point of view, there's no problem at all. They are not breaking any laws and they like hanging out in the parking lot. Their motivation is to meet friends, have fun, show off, and act cool.

> The proprietors may have made the false assumption that these kids are beyond their control and influence as there is the very real barrier that they cannot prosecute them or involve the law. They are not criminals.

But in revisiting the core motivators there is an opportunity to extend the sphere of influence.

These kids think the parking lot is a cool place. How can that be changed?

> The owners started to play very uncool, "easy-listening" music through speakers outside the store.

> The kids soon went elsewhere.

7. The Ideascape: How to explore your mind

Sometimes, while investigating and redefining a problem, we'll stumble upon the solution. We'll get lucky and it will just occur to us.

On other occasions we'll look at the problem every which way and still not see how to solve it. At such moments, we need an inductive as opposed to a deductive thought process. Analysis, logic, and reason —these tools alone aren't doing the job. Somehow we need to take a creative leap and find a new approach.

There are many "Creative Thinking Tools" we can use to help us do this. "Brainstorming" is probably the most popular, and has been since the 1950s. And given a clear understanding of the problem and the right people in the room, it's often very effective.

Unfortunately, the original approach to Brainstorming is rarely used or taught. And so it has devolved over the years with not many people knowing how to do it well. A successful outcome requires more than a whiteboard and someone willing to write down the group's ideas and suggestions. (We'll look at how we can improve our technique in Chapter 8.)

More recently we've seen creative tools developed by such innovative thinkers as Edward de Bono and Tony Buzan.

De Bono coined the phrase "Lateral Thinking" and has invented many effective techniques to promote divergent as opposed to convergent thinking.

Tony Buzan developed the MindMap as a way of helping schoolchildren retain information better while studying for exams. It was some time later that he discovered its potential for generating great ideas.

Genrich Altshuller, an inventor working in the patent department of the Russian Navy in the 1940s, developed a creative thinking system we now call SIT—Systematic Inventive Thinking. He studied over 200,000 patents in order to develop a concept that would facilitate idea generation. In his words, "You can wait a hundred years for enlightenment or you can solve the problem in 15 minutes with these principles."

These are just a few of the many techniques that have been designed to help us "think outside the box." When I Googled "Creative Thinking Tools" I received 12.7 million results in 0.12 seconds. (How's that for Accelerated Evolution?)

But as with any toolbox, the problem isn't just knowing how to use the tool. You have to know which tool to use.

As far as I know, **there is no "one size fits all" approach to creative thinking problems**. No one has yet designed a Swiss Army Brain with a set of tools that fold out for any and every occasion.

In the workshops we run, I usually explain this predicament with this analogy.

Creative thinking techniques are rather like basic self-defense techniques.

Over the years, I've had a number of friends sign up for self-defense classes where they go to learn some form of Judo or Karate. Usually, after a session or two, they come back and suggest I attack them with a rolled-up magazine or newspaper so that they can show off their new streetfighting skills.

This has never proven to be much of a challenge. I just take the "weapon," prod them directly in the chest, and say, "You're dead!" Their response invariably goes something like this: "No! You have to hold the newspaper up high and come toward me making a downward stabbing motion." (Or some other clearly defined approach.) I always stop at this point because I know I'm going to get my arm bent.

Basic self-defense tactics work very well when you can anticipate the exact nature of the attack.

Creative Thinking Tools work very well when you can anticipate the exact nature of the solution.

Creative solutions always seem pitifully simple in retrospect. It's always easy to see how a creative tool would have taken us to the now blindingly obvious answer.

But it's not so easy when you are looking forward. When you have no idea of where the solution may lie, how do you choose a tool to guide your thoughts in the right direction?

This is where Ideascape can help.

Once you have reached the "Defined Problem," Ideascape can give you an insight into which tools might help you solve it.

Ideascape is a system or process that is built on a metaphor.

It describes your mind as an inner world that has four regions. When we get "stuck" trying to solve a problem, we are caught up or lost in one of these four regions or mental spaces.

I've called them The Ocean, The Forest, The Desert, and The City.

The only way to understand them is to go there. So we're going to use some problems and riddles to take a tour of the four regions. You'll find some are more familiar than others. But once you learn to recognize where you are, you can experiment with the thinking tools that are designed for each region. (We'll get to the tools later.)

So take a blank sheet of paper and try to solve the following 12 problems. If you get stuck, try and understand how you are feeling about the problem. Make a few notes about the mental struggle you are experiencing.

For example, you might feel stumped with absolutely no idea how to get started on the problem. Or you might feel confused. Or you might feel frustrated, as you are tantalizingly close to a solution but can't quite make it work.

You'll find that even if your thoughts grind to a halt, your feelings won't.

Even when you don't know what to think, you'll still know what and how you are feeling. So write those feelings down along with your answers.

Research shows that most people solve Brainteasers in the first two minutes or not at all. After that time has passed, the mind has usually made assumptions it regards as incontrovertible truths. We then get stuck in a neural pathway that repeatedly leads us to either the wrong conclusion or nowhere at all.

But if you do get stuck for longer than a couple of minutes, stick with it. Persist with each problem until you can see how you are thinking and feeling.

PROBLEM No. 1: The Light Switches

You are in a room where there are three light switches on the wall. You know that each switch turns on a light in the room next door. But you can't see into that room. Your challenge is to work out which switch controls which light. But you can only go into the room next door once.

How do you do it?

PROBLEM No. 2: The Glacier

An explorer is traversing a glacier in the Arctic Circle when he comes across two bodies that have been caught and buried in the ice flow. He carefully exhumes them—a man and a woman. They are both completely naked and they are carrying absolutely nothing with them. Their bodies bear no scars or signs of injury. They are perfectly preserved.

How does the explorer immediately know they are the ancient bodies of Adam and Eve?

PROBLEM No. 3: The Rope Ladder

A boat is sitting in the harbor when the captain throws a rope ladder overboard. The ladder has ten rungs and two of them go beneath the surface of the water. The rungs are nine inches apart. The tide is rising at the rate of 18 inches per hour.

How many rungs will be under the water when two hours have passed?

PROBLEM No. 4: The Wife and Daughter

Two men are drinking in a pub when a woman and a girl come into the bar. One man turns around and sees them and then says to his friend, "I'd better get going, my wife and daughter have just come in." His friend turns around and sees the same woman and girl and says, "Yes, my wife and daughter have just arrived too."

How can this be true?

PROBLEM No. 5: The Fly

A man and a woman are standing ten feet apart. They begin to walk toward one another. They walk at a steady pace of one foot every ten seconds.

> There is a fly sitting on the woman's nose. As they begin to walk the fly takes off and flies directly to the man's nose, lands on it, and then without hesitating takes off again and flies back to the woman's nose. The fly travels at a constant speed of one foot per second. The fly travels back and forth in this way while the man and woman continue to approach one another.

The fly's trips get shorter as the couple get closer and closer together.
> So how far does the fly travel before the man's nose and the woman's nose are touching and it has nowhere left to go?

PROBLEM No. 6: The Alarm Clock

A woman is caring for her elderly husband who has a heart problem. She has to give him medicine in the middle of the night but finds it difficult to wake up at the appropriate time. So she decides to set an alarm clock.

> That night her husband is sleeping and dreams that he is a bomb disposal expert working for the counter-terrorism division of the army. In his dream he is defusing a bomb that has an alarm clock on it. Just as the second hand ticks to the point where the bomb will go off, his wife's alarm clock in the bedroom rings very loudly. The shock of his dream appearing to be real and that he is about to be blown to smithereens gives him a heart attack and he dies.

His wife is grief-stricken and feels terribly guilty but her friends refuse to believe her story. Why?

PROBLEM No. 7: The Nine Dots

●　　●　　●

●　　●　　●

●　　●　　●

Join the nine dots with four straight lines with your pen never leaving the page.
If you already know how to do this problem, join the
dots with three straight lines but you are allowed to let
your pen leave the page once only.

PROBLEM No. 8: The Silent Assassin

A man goes to the movies with his wife. During the course of the movie he is suddenly
gripped by a jealous rage and strangles her. There are at least a hundred people in the
audience but none of them pay any attention to this hideous event. At the end of the
film, the husband manages to get his wife's body out of the cinema without being
noticed or stopped by either the other audience members or the management.
How did he do it?

PROBLEM No. 9: The Fishing Rods

Two fathers and two sons go out on a shopping expedition to buy fishing
rods. They visit a large sporting store but find that it only has three rods
left. But they are perfectly happy. They each leave the store with a rod.
How is this possible?

PROBLEM No. 10: The Equation

Look at this equation:

$$2 + 7 - 118 = 129$$

As you can see, it's wrong. How can you make this equation correct by adding a single straight line? If you think you already know how to do this, keep trying. There are three ways in all. Maybe more.

PROBLEM No. 11: The Two Strings

You are in an empty room where two pieces of string are hanging from the ceiling. They are just far enough apart that you can't reach one while holding the other.

Your challenge is to join the pieces of string together. The following items have been placed on the floor to help you. A stick of chewing gum, a pair of scissors, and a glass of water.

How do you do it?

PROBLEM No. 12: The Fraudster

A man goes to a collector of antiquities to show him a very rare and valuable coin he has acquired. It's from the Roman era, dated 17 BC, heavily encrusted and scarred but clearly engraved with an image that was frequently found on coins of that age.

Why does the collector immediately call the police and report the man as a fraudster?

Before we go to the answers, let's look closely at the four different regions of the Ideascape and see if we recognize them after struggling through these puzzles.

The Ocean

Imagine an expanse of ocean that is far from the shore. In every direction you look, you see nothing. The skies are blue and cloudless, the sun is directly overhead, there's no trace of wind, and the seas are calm. You can detect no current in the water. There are no hints to suggest the direction you must take to find the safety of dry land.

Now imagine that this is actually a state of mind. You are stranded. Becalmed. Your thoughts have no obvious direction to follow. Nothing pushes or pulls you in any particular direction. You look around and see nothing—just a vast emptiness.

Did you experience a version of this when solving any of the 12 problems? At any time, did you have a sense of being lost? None of the information in the problem gave you a sense of where the solution might lie?

Some people find this with the problem of the Silent Assassin. There is nothing to suggest how this event could possibly have taken place without the other filmgoers taking notice or getting involved. Similarly, in the Glacier, the evidence seems to have been stripped of any clues. Naked bodies? What can they reveal?

If you experienced this sense of bewilderment, we're going to say you were lost on the Ocean, a vast sea of endless possibilities but no obvious opportunities.

The Forest

The Forest is a very different experience. In a sense, it's the exact opposite of how we feel in the Ocean.

> Imagine a forest that is densely overgrown. You can see nothing but trees and trees behind trees. There are paths but no signposts and no suggestion of a clearing anywhere nearby. This leaves you without a point of reference. If you start walking, it will be difficult to find your way back.

If we think of this as a state of mind, then the Forest represents an overabundance of information and possible paths to follow. The trouble is, we tend to go round and round and all the paths start to look the same. We become trapped and feel we "can't see the forest for the trees." After a while, we get tired. Circling thought is frustrating and if we don't find a solution the situation starts to feel hopeless.

> Some people get caught up in the Forest when trying to solve the riddle of the two women being the wife and daughter of two different men. At first the problem would seem to lie simply in finding the relationship from within a limited number of possibilities. And, in fact, this is so. But until you make a conceptual leap, the obvious possibilities will keep recurring and leading nowhere.

> The emotional experience of being in the Forest is one of being trapped, stifled by circling thoughts that never lead to a solution.

The Desert

The desert is a barren, featureless, and empty place. The dunes have an undulating, amorphous similarity. One looks pretty much like another. And we can't use them to orient ourselves as they are constantly shifting.

> In the desert, without any landmarks and sense of direction, the mind can start to play tricks on us.

> A mirage, even if we know it to be illusory, can be very seductive. When we can see nowhere else to go, the shimmering sense of a refuge we know to be false becomes hard to abandon. It seems better than nothing because it's the only thing.

The Desert of the Ideascape is one in which we become attached to a solution that doesn't work. A mirage solution. Even though we know it probably will never work, we find it hard to discard. We keep trying to make it work.

> The nine dots test often leads people into this region. In workshops, I have found test sheets where people have gone over the same dots again and again. They are toying with a solution that is not quite working and are holding onto the vain hope that, if they try it one more time, it might suddenly come good.

> It never does.

Perversely, we know when a solution is not going to work. But in the Desert, we feel compelled to keep trying it.

The City

Of all the Ideascape regions, the City is perhaps the easiest to visualize and one of the most frequently visited. Imagine a city where the traffic has ground to a halt. Gridlock.

> There are many different routes and roads available but the density of the traffic is such that none of them can take you anywhere. You're stuck.

This form of information overload is a common blockage to creative thinking.

> And frequently, in the frustration and confusion, we don't notice the shortcut we could take which would bypass much of the information that is clogging up our neural pathways.

> The Fly problem often leads to the City. There is the opportunity to reach the answer through a very complex, brain-aching set of calculations. But the answer lies in a shortcut that renders such thoughts unnecessary.

Complexity is the enemy of creative thinking. Most ideas come from simple but precise observations and associations. And so we must learn to recognize the City and find our way out of it.

> You might get a better sense of the Ideascape regions by looking at the answers. Let's go through them.

PROBLEM No. 1: The Light Switches

The solution is to turn on one light switch and then leave it on for a while. Then turn it off and turn on a different light. Now go immediately into the room. One of the bulbs will be on. You know which switch controls that one—you've just flicked it. And one of the bulbs will be hot. The other will be cold. You know the hot one was controlled by the first switch you flicked. So you now know all three.

> For some, this might be an Ocean problem. There are so few clues it is hard to know where to start. But there is information in the wording of the problem and closer examination might have given us a direction. We'll look at how we might do that later.

PROBLEM No. 2: The Glacier

> The bodies had no belly buttons. Again, with this problem there is a distinct lack of information to guide us. It reminds me a little of Sherlock Holmes' "Strange case of the dog in the night-time." There, the clue was that the dog didn't bark. It was the absence of an event that proved significant. Similarly, in this problem it is the absence of something that enables us to understand the event and come to a solution.

PROBLEM No. 3: The Rope Ladder

This problem seems to take different people to different regions of the Ideascape. Some will see it as a mathematical problem and when told that their answer is incorrect will continue to search for the right number by checking their calculations. That could be a mirage in the Desert or just the circling thoughts one finds in the Forest.

> Others will immediately realize that boats float and that the ladder will rise at the same rate as the tide. After two hours, only two rungs will still be under the water.

PROBLEM No. 4: The Wife and Daughter

> I found this problem very difficult. During my attempts to solve it, I think I visited the Forest and the City. The same thoughts seem to be going around and around and I felt gridlocked with the information provided.

The answer is that each man had a daughter by a previous marriage and they then married each other's daughter. Still in gridlock? Try writing it out on a piece of paper.

PROBLEM No. 5: The Fly

For some this is a classic City problem. There is enough information to try to calculate this solution the hard way. It would take a genius mind to do it. As each journey gets shorter the complexities pile upon complexities.

> The shortcut is to ask how long will it take for the couple to meet nose to nose. As they are both walking toward each other at a rate of one foot every ten seconds, they get closer by two feet every ten seconds. They are ten feet apart so it will take them 50 seconds to touch.

The fly is traveling at a constant speed of one foot per second. He's going to fly for 50 seconds. He'll travel 50 feet.

> No complex, mind-jamming mathematics required.

PROBLEM No. 6: The Alarm Clock

This can seem obvious. To some, but not to me. As I believed that it could actually happen, it never occurred to me that there is no way we could know it had happened.

> That is why her friends refuse to believe her story. It's impossible for her to have known what her husband was dreaming as he died before he could tell her.

PROBLEM No. 7: The Dots

This is an old puzzle and one that many people regard as the origin of the phrase, "Think outside the Box." They may be right although I suspect the metaphor comes from a quote by Einstein in which he said, "A problem cannot be solved with the same kind of thinking which created it."

> But that's a moot point.

> The fact remains that to solve the puzzle you need to draw outside the box. Then it's quite easy, as you can see from the illustration.

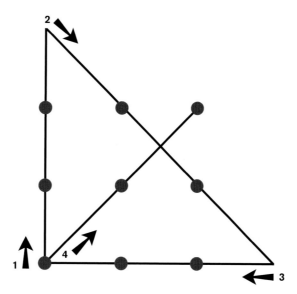

For those of you who knew this puzzle I suggested that you try to connect the dots with three lines with your pen leaving the page only once. To the best of my knowledge this is impossible and I apologize for any time you spent in vain. I just wanted to push you into one of the Ideascape terrains so that you could recognize it later.

However, there are other ways of solving this puzzle.

Two of them came up in a workshop I was running.

The first requires you to shrink the image on a photocopier and then use a very thick magic marker. In this way you can join all the dots with a single line. That's definitely possible.

The second requires you to join the first vertical line of dots and then walk all the way around the world re-entering the room just a few millimeters to the right and then join the middle line of dots. One further circumnavigation of the planet and you've done it. It might be a challenging process that requires a great deal of time, energy, and ink but it's a great piece of conceptual thinking.

PROBLEM No. 8: The Silent Assassin

If you had difficulty solving this problem you'll find your assumptions are probably the reason why. If you assume that the cinema is an enclosed space with people sitting beside one another, you'll struggle to imagine how this could have taken place. Most likely, you'll end up on the Ocean and feel completely "at sea."

But if you challenge that assumption and ask where else might they be watching a film together you might hit upon the idea that they were at a drive-in movie theater.

Suddenly, all is explained.

PROBLEM No. 9: The Fishing Rods

There's plenty of information in this riddle, but it's possible to get trapped in the Forest and go round and round with it. Or you may find that the information is unhelpful and leads nowhere.

> The answer is that there are three people. A son, his father, and his father's father or grandfather. That makes two fathers and two sons between the three of them. One rod each.

PROBLEM No. 10: The Equation

> The temptation is to get stuck in the Forest and see this as a mathematical problem. But the answer is more visual than numerical.

With one straight line

$$2+7 - 118 = 129$$

can become

$$247 - 118 = 129$$

> This equation is then correct.
> There are two alternatives that I have seen. One is to put a strike through the equals sign so that it reads $2 + 7 - 118 \neq 129$. The other is to modify the equals sign so that it reads $2 + 7 - 118 \geq 129$.

PROBLEM No. 11: The Two Strings

There are many versions of this problem on the Internet. All of them offer different objects to help you solve the problem.

> That alone tells you that the exact nature of the objects may not be relevant. And this is the case. We take this problem to one of the Ideascape regions and get stuck there because we assume the scissors are for cutting or the gum is for chewing and gluing, and the water, well who knows what the glass of water is for.

The answer is that you tie the scissors to one piece of string and set it swinging like a pendulum. You can then position yourself to hold the other piece and wait for the scissors to swing toward you. When you catch the scissors you can then tie the strings together.

PROBLEM No. 12: The Fraudster

It's impossible for a coin to be dated 17 BC. Seventeen years before Christ was born, no one knew he was going to be born—hence the fraud.

The clue in this case is clearly within the problem but noticing it requires an uncommon presence of mind. This is frequently a difficulty with the Ocean and we'll look at a technique to help overcome it.

So, apart from a little neurobic exercise, what have we gained from the process of solving these problems?

The Ideascape hasn't been designed to help you solve riddles and lateral thinking problems. These Brainteasers are usually written and phrased very carefully to hide the solution. They are intended to trick you.

But the process of struggling with them is useful if it helps you identify and recognize the characteristics of the four regions of the Ideascape.

The four terrains don't categorize the problem, they categorize your response to the problem. Or more specifically, they categorize the particular way in which you are feeling stuck.

There are several different types of "stuck." Distinguishing one from another is the first step in knowing what to do about it.

8. The Creative Compass

It's not always easy to navigate your way through the Ideascape.

Sometimes you may not know where you are.

The borders between one region and the next often overlap. This means you could find yourself in two regions at the same time. Or sometimes you might escape one region and then get caught up immediately in another.

And if you are working with a team of people, you may find that they are all in different regions while working on the same problem.

None of this really matters.

The real purpose of the Ideascape is to keep your thoughts flowing. **The true enemy of creative thinking is no thinking**. When the mind grinds to a halt or starts spinning its wheels and coming up with the same ideas over and over again, then we stand little chance of finding a new and interesting solution to the problem we are trying to solve.

Where are we now? How is this problem affecting me now? Don't be concerned with how it was affecting you before or how it might be affecting someone else.

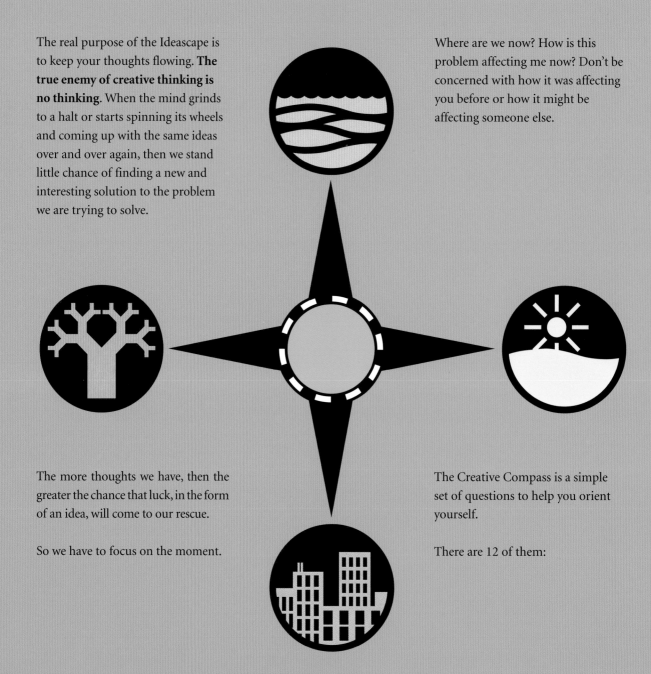

The more thoughts we have, then the greater the chance that luck, in the form of an idea, will come to our rescue.

So we have to focus on the moment.

The Creative Compass is a simple set of questions to help you orient yourself.

There are 12 of them:

1. **Do I feel lost?**
(Do I lack direction and not know where to start?)

2. **Do I feel clueless?**
(Are there no hints as to where the solution might lie?)

3. **Do I feel adrift?**
(My mind has failed to engage with the problem and is not moving with any purpose.)

4. **Do I feel trapped?**
(Are the same thoughts going around and around in my head?)

5. **Do I feel overwhelmed?**
(Have I lost perspective? Can I not see the forest for the trees?)

6. **Do I feel bewildered?**
(Many thoughts but I'm making no progress.)

7. **Do I feel tricked?**
(I can see a solution that ought to work but it doesn't work.)

8. **Do I feel spellbound?**
(I'm stuck on a thought process that is tantalizingly close to working. But I know it won't.)

9. **Do I feel hopeless?**
(The only solution I can see is clearly not going to work.)

10. **Do I feel overloaded?**
(There's too much information and I don't know where to start.)

11. **Do I feel stuck?**
(My mind has ground to a halt.)

12. **Do I feel frustrated?**
(I know I've taken a wrong turn and got stuck in the details.)

All of these questions ask, "Do I feel…?"

We're trying to use what I call Compass Emotions.

When our thoughts are in a mess, our feelings might give us a better sense of where we are with the problem.

If you answer "Yes" to questions 1–3, you are probably having some sort of Ocean experience.

"Yes" to questions 4–6 and it looks as if you are going round and around in the Forest.

Being mesmerized by a solution that doesn't work will probably make you check one or more of the boxes in questions 7–9. This will put you in the Desert.

And if you answered "Yes" to questions 10–12, your mind has most likely ground to a halt in the City.

A quick thumbnail version of this test would look like this:

Lost	=	The Ocean
Trapped	=	The Forest
Tricked	=	The Desert
Paralyzed	=	The City

Once we have established where we are, we can start to make our plans for escape. There are different routes out of each of the terrains and different tools to help us find them.

Let's break it down region by region.

The Ocean

To get out of the ocean we need to create movement. We need to choose a direction. And any direction is better than no direction. We have two options.

We can arbitrarily set sail and see where it takes us. This is not as hopeless as it sounds. Once we start moving our perspective will change and features will appear on the horizon. Eventually, our thoughts will find a direction. Or we can look under the surface of the problem and see if there are some clues hiding there.

(This works particularly well with brainteasers as they are written to confuse us, lay false trails, and inspire incorrect assumptions.).

To escape the Ocean, we need to become Explorers.

The Forest

The Forest is full of information and full of pathways through it. Trouble is, none of them is leading anywhere interesting.

One option is to leave the existing paths and hack a new one through the undergrowth. The information will be the same, but we'll be moving through it in a new direction. We'll cross our old paths at a new and different angle and maybe find our way to a new destination.

Alternatively, we can find a way of changing our perspective. How can we see the same old information with new eyes? If we could develop a bird's eye view of the Forest we might be able to see our way out of it.

To escape the Forest, we need to change our point of view.

The Desert

A mirage may fool us for a minute or two but we'll quickly discover that this solution isn't going to work. The sooner we abandon it the better. If we continue in this direction we'll exhaust ourselves and eventually give up.

We could strike out into the unknown and walk into the vast emptiness of the dunes in the hope of finding a new path. Just pick any direction that doesn't take us to the mirage. We'd find ourselves in a sandy version of the Ocean. This is no bad thing and definitely an option we'll explore.

Or we could retrace our steps. If we walk backward we'll get closer to the problem but approach it from a different angle. We may notice some paths that we didn't take along the way.

To escape the Desert, we need to defy our inclinations and turn around.

The City

It's the overwhelming complexity of thoughts that paralyzes us in the City. There's too much information and much of it is probably irrelevant or unnecessary. To find a way through we need to experiment with knowing less. Metaphorically, we can do that by taking an empty road. Maybe we can then work our way back around and find a less congested path to the solution.

Or we could try and find a parallel path. One that is not congested with our facts and assumptions. Perhaps we can see how someone else found a way through a similar complexity. Their route might work for us.

To escape the City we need to simplify.

This gives us four basic approaches to navigating our way around the Ideascape.

We can throw caution to the wind and explore; we can change our point of view; we can turn around and go back in the direction from where we came; or we can reduce the congestion by simplifying the problem.

Now let's look at the tools that can put these strategies into practice.

9. Cerebral Software: the Ideascape Toolkit

Once we know where we are stranded in the Ideascape, we're in a position to do something about it. As we've seen, each region requires a particular escape strategy if we're going to get some new thoughts and ideas flowing.

We're now going to look at a set of tools that will help us put these strategies into action. I use the word "tools" as the term has become idiomatic within the business of creative thinking. But I think cerebral software is probably a better analogy.

Think of these tools as applications or widgets. Each one is designed to help our brains (our CPUs) find different ways of processing the information that is contained within a problem.

Unlike most software packages, none of these guarantees an outcome. The results will never be predictable. As is always the case with creative thinking, luck will play a crucial role.

But **with the right tool, we can load the dice in our favor.** We can give our "prepared mind" a better chance of encountering and recognizing the "Trigger" moments we studied in Chapter 5.

There are two tools for each region.

The Ocean

As we have seen, the greatest difficulty in being lost on the Ocean is that we are becalmed. We are not going anywhere because there is nothing on the horizon to suggest which way we should set sail. There are no winds blowing.

But if our strategy is to explore, we need to get moving. And any direction is better than no direction.

To do this, we're going to use a tool we'll call Fishing.

I have always thought that fishing is a good analogy for creative thinking. Both require a combination of skill and luck. And patience.

The skill is in knowing where you should set your rod, where the fish are likely to be jumping, knowing their feeding hours and what sort of bait attracts them. But even armed with all this knowledge, you can still spend a day on the riverbank and reel in weeds and old boots. On another day, in the same spot, you'll pull out a prizewinner.

You just have to trust your luck.

But one thing is certain. You won't catch a fish unless you keep casting your line. The Fishing tool is designed to do just this. It uses random words as bait to help us attract ideas.

It's extremely simple to use. Just write down your Defined Problem and then open a dictionary and pick a word. Any word. Preferably, the first word you see as long as you understand what it means. (There is absolutely no point in trying to look for a "good" word or one that you imagine is going to be particularly helpful.)

Then write that word next to the problem.

The juxtaposition will probably look and feel uncomfortable. Good. Your challenge is to force a connection between the problem and anything you might associate with the word you have chosen. You need to build a bridge of thoughts that connects one to the other.

In doing this, two things will immediately start to happen.

First, you'll start to move. The random word will act as a false landmark on your horizon and you'll start to sail in that direction. You're no longer in the doldrums.

Second, you'll be surprised to find that other landmarks immediately start to appear. And because these landmarks have been created in reference to the problem you are trying to solve, many if not all of them will be relevant.

This is where you need to keep your eyes peeled because any of these new landmarks or thoughts could take you to a Trigger moment.

Referring back to Arthur Koestler, what you are doing is forcing the "intersection of two matrices of thought."

New ideas can be created by this collision of the relevant and the random.

Edward de Bono cites a very clear example is his book *Po: Beyond Yes and No*. He was working with a team of designers and he asked them to modify a soda siphon so that the user would know when it was about to run out of water. The siphon was made of thick metal and so the waterline was completely invisible.

(You'll be familiar with this problem if you've decided to cook a BBQ and then realized you don't know how much gas is left in the bottle. Picking it up and shaking it only gives you the vaguest notion of whether it's going to run out before the sausages are cooked to perfection.)

The designers came back with some suggestions but none of them was practical. It would be too expensive to fit glass panels or pressure valves. The brief required a solution that wouldn't price the siphons out of the market.

They then reconsidered the problem but added a random word.

"Earring."

Building a bridge to this unconnected thought led to a new and very interesting solution.

The designers suggested that a floating ball be suspended inside the tank. It would be attached to a chain that was one inch shorter than the height of the tank.

When the tank is full, the ball will float on the surface of the water. But when the level drops to less than one inch, the ball will swing on the end of the chain and bang against the sides, giving us an audible signal. When we hear it, we know we have less than one inch of water left.

Cheap, simple to install, and effective.

"Earring" had been picked at random from the dictionary. But the process of forcing it to become relevant created a Trigger. Earrings hang from the ear and this suggested the possibility of hanging something inside the siphon.

I've used Fishing in many creative workshops and it's one of the most popular and effective tools because it always gets the mind moving and helps generate new ideas. Many of them get thrown back in, but there are many more where those came from.

The Soda Siphon

Here are the four steps to using the tool:

1. **Write out the Defined Problem.**
2. **Pick a word at random from a dictionary.**
3. **Write the word beneath the problem.**
4. **Create connections between the word and the problem and see what new thoughts and ideas occur.**

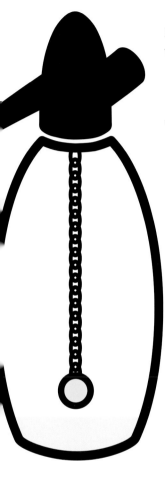

If Fishing doesn't deliver any usable thoughts and ideas, it might be worth taking a closer look at the problem.

We get stranded on the Ocean when we feel there are no clues to suggest a direction for our thoughts. But perhaps we've overlooked something.

"Diving" is the other tool we can use when lost on the Ocean.

It's a process that takes us beneath the surface of the problem and helps us search for two things—assumptions and associations.

Looking back at the 12 Brainteasers we tried to solve in Chapter 7, it's clear that assumptions frequently inhibit our thinking. In nearly all of those problems a false assumption was responsible for the difficulty we encountered. And sometimes just uncovering the assumption will give us a Trigger.

So we need a rigorous process for weeding them out. At the same time we need to see if we can create connections and intersections between the many associations that are attached to the words of the problem.

This is a very mechanistic approach. Its virtue is that is leaves few stones unturned.

Again, it's very simple.

Write out the Defined Problem. Use as few words as possible but don't compromise the meaning. We need an absolutely clear understanding of the issue we are trying to resolve.

Then remove any words that are not absolutely germane to the issue—the ifs, ands, buts, and so on. Anything that appears irrelevant. But be careful.

As an example let's look back at the problem of the Fishing Rods. I've seen many people end up on the Ocean with this one.

Here is how we stated it originally:

Two fathers and two sons go out on a shopping expedition to buy fishing rods. They visit a large sporting store but find that it only has three rods left. But they are perfectly happy. They each leave the store with a rod.

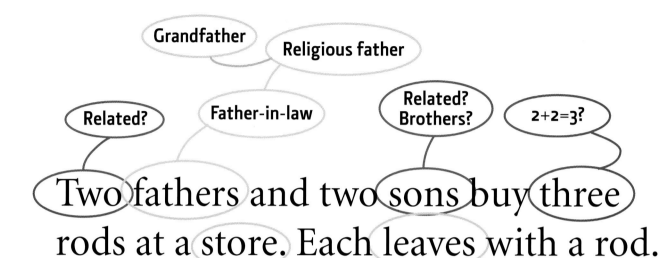

Here's the version for Diving:

Two fathers and two sons buy three rods at a store. Each leaves with a rod.

You'll notice that by reducing the problem we've given it a sharper focus. Now circle the individual words or chunks of meaning and create a spidergram as shown above.

Start with assumptions. Challenge every assumption you might be making. Use one color pen to do that.

For example, you might question the assumption you are making about the relationship between the fathers and the sons. Are they in fact related? What other possible relationships could exist?

Or you might challenge your assumption about "store." Is it a place where things are sold or is it a place where things are kept? Does this suggest any new thoughts?

When you have doggedly worked your way through assumptions, go looking for associations. Use a different color.

What do you associate with the idea of two fathers?

What do you associate with a store? If you look at the spidergram I've started to fill out, you'll see stores suggest special offers and discounts. Maybe there is a Trigger here. They bought three rods and "got one free" on a special deal. Not an elegant solution but a possibility.

It might even be that the associations around "three" eventually connect with the associations around "fathers." That might lead to the Trigger of considering there are only three people. Who knows?

But one thing we do know. We are no longer drifting listlessly on the Ocean. We are moving.

Diving forces us to challenge assumptions, create associations and connections, and give ourselves a better chance of getting lucky.

Here are the five steps for using the tool:
1. **Write out the Defined Problem.**
2. **Pare it down by cutting out unnecessary words.**
3. **Create a spidergram that challenges the assumptions around all the key words.**
4. **Create a second spidergram that allows key word associations to radiate outward.**
5. **Look for connections around the outer edge of the spidergram.**

The Forest

Searching for clues and information is not a problem we face when we are trapped in the Forest. Far from it. We are surrounded by them.

Our difficulty comes from habit and familiarity. If we are in the Forest we are likely to have seen the trees and paths many times before. And, out of force of habit, we use the same paths to get though them. Trouble is, they don't lead us anywhere new and interesting. We either go nowhere or end up back where we started.

Trailblazing is a tool that helps us reprocess information so that we can create new paths and, one hopes, find some new solutions.

It's based on a concept that goes by the unwieldy name of Morphological Forced Connections.

The first step is to look at the attributes of the Defined Problem.

As an example we'll use a recruitment issue: "How do we attract talented sales staff to regional sales without paying over the odds?"

Five variable attributes might be: The salespeople we target, the pay we offer, the benefits we offer, the hours we require them to work, and the method by which we recruit them. Then we ask ourselves, what are our current methods?

In this case the answer might be:

We target younger and less experienced staff, we offer them commission and retainer, they get the benefit of an expense account, we require them to work full time, and we recruit from within the industry.

We now organize this information as a Trailblazing matrix. It will look like this:

HOW TO ATTRACT TALENTED SALES STAFF TO REGIONAL SALES WITHOUT PAYING OVER THE ODDS?

Attributes	Target Salespeople	Pay Offered	Benefits Offered	Hours Required	Recruiting method
Current Methods	Younger end Less exp	Commission & Retainer	Expense Account	Full Time	From Industry
Alternatives					
Alternatives					
Alternatives					
Alternatives					
Alternatives					

We now work vertically to list all the alternatives to our current methods. Work from top to bottom and from left to right. It might end up looking something like the diagram below.

Once the matrix is fully populated we can start to Trailblaze by making connections laterally across the columns. New combinations will immediately lead to new ideas.

HOW TO ATTRACT TALENTED SALES STAFF TO REGIONAL SALES WITHOUT PAYING OVER THE ODDS?

Attributes	Target Salespeople	Pay Offered	Benefits Offered	Hours Required	Recruiting method
Current Methods	Younger end Less exp	Commission & Retainer	Expense Account	Full Time	From Industry
Alternatives	Mothers Returning	Higher	All Car Expenses	Part Time	Headhunter
Alternatives	Old Hands	Lower	Offer Accommodation	Match Student Hours	Advertise
Alternatives	Other industry Experts	Cash only	Exotic Vacations	Shift Work	Club
Alternatives	Students	Commission only	Day Care	Mostly Nights & Weekends	Campuses/ Schools
Alternatives	Retirees	Goods and Services	Clothes	After School	Radio

Here are two examples:

The Forest–Trailblazing

HOW TO ATTRACT TALENTED SALES STAFF TO REGIONAL SALES WITHOUT PAYING OVER THE ODDS?

Attributes	Target Salespeople	Pay Offered	Benefits Offered	Hours Required	Recruiting method
Current Methods	Younger end Less exp	Commission & Retainer	Expense Account	Full Time	From Industry
Alternatives	Mothers Returning	Higher	All Car Expenses	Part Time	Headhunter
Alternatives	Old Hands	Lower	Offer Accommodation	Match Student Hours	Advertise
Alternatives	Other industry Experts	Cash only	Exotic Vacations	Shift Work	Club
Alternatives	Students	Commission only	Day Care	Mostly Nights & Weekends	Campuses/ Schools
Alternatives	Retirees	Goods and Services	Clothes	After School	Radio

Attributes	Target Salespeople	Pay Offered	Benefits Offered	Hours Required	Recruiting method
Current Methods	Younger end Less exp	Commission & Retainer	Expense Account	Full Time	From Industry
Alternatives	Mothers Returning	Higher	All Car Expenses	Part Time	Headhunter
Alternatives	Old Hands	Lower	Offer Accommodation	Match Student Hours	Advertise
Alternatives	Other industry Experts	Cash only	Exotic Vacations	Shift Work	Club
Alternatives	Students	Commission only	Day Care	Mostly Nights & Weekends	Campuses/ Schools
Alternatives	Retirees	Goods and Services	Clothes	After School	Radio

One great strength of the Trailblazing process is that it allows you to fill the matrix with variables that are within the bounds of possibility. So, although the connections are random, arbitrary, and unexpected, there is a good chance that the ideas produced will be feasible.

Many creative thinking tools or techniques generate too many ideas that are way beyond what is possible. And although these crazy ideas may well be the stepping stones to practical ideas, there is still some way to go.

But in one process, Trailblazing can let you reorganize the trees and create new paths through the Forest.

Here are five steps for using the tool:
1. **Write out the Defined Problem.**
2. **Create a matrix and arrange the attributes of the problem across the top row.**
3. **Write the current method beneath each attribute.**
4. **List alternative methods beneath each current method.**
5. **When the matrix is full, Trailblaze by making connections laterally.**

Another way we might change our point of view to escape the Forest is to temporarily become someone else.

Some years ago I had a boss who had the irritating habit of repeating the same joke. I'd ask his help with some problem that was troubling me and he'd say, "Nick, ask yourself. What would a smart guy do in your situation?"

Over the years, I've come to realize it's not such a stupid question. (I'm not sure he's ever realized that.) If we could borrow someone else's thought processes, we'd see different trees and different paths.

We have a tool to help us do that. It's called Headhunting.

Quite simply, this means we're going to borrow someone else's head, pop it on, and then look at the situation through their eyes. A new set of neural pathways will appear.

This is surprisingly easy to do.

Take a blank sheet of paper and, in about 15 seconds, write down as many answers as you can to this question.

"Why did the cow jump over the moon?"

Now answer the same question again, but not as yourself. Instead imagine you are Mother Teresa. What answer might she give?

Take another 15 seconds.

When you've done that, repeat the process until you have answered the same question through the eyes of everyone on this list.

Leonardo da Vinci	**The Man with No Name**
Mother Teresa	**Al Capone**
Hitler	**Gandalf**
Homer Simpson	**Snow White**
Casanova	**Scott of the Antarctic**
Bob Hope	**The Dalai Lama**

You'll find that entirely different, albeit absurd, explanations occur to you. It is in fact very easy to see the world through other people's eyes.

Particularly these people. The list is not random or arbitrary. I've chosen characters that represent the 12 different Jungian archetypes.

Carl Jung believed that we come into the world with an innate understanding of 12 personalities he described as:

The Creator	**The Hero**
The Caregiver	**The Outlaw**
The Ruler	**The Magician**
The Regular Guy	**The Innocent**
The Lover	**The Explorer**
The Jester	**The Sage**

Because we instinctively know their personalities, it's easy for us to get inside their heads.

The chart opposite gives you some guidelines and characteristics to remind you how these archetypes behave, what they desire, and what they fear.

THE CAREGIVER

MOTTO:
Love your neighbor as yourself

DESIRE:
To protect people from harm

STRATEGY:
To do things for others

THE CREATOR

MOTTO:
If it can be imagined,
it can be created

DESIRE:
To create something of enduring value

STRATEGY:
To develop artistic control and skill

THE EXPLORER

MOTTO:
Don't fence me in

DESIRE:
The freedom to explore the self
and the world

STRATEGY:
Escape, seek new experiences

THE HERO

MOTTO:
Where there's a will, there's a way

DESIRE:
To prove one's worth through
courage

STRATEGY:
To become strong and powerful

THE INNOCENT

MOTTO:
Free to be you and to be me

DESIRE:
To experience paradise

STRATEGY:
To do things properly and fairly

THE JESTER

MOTTO:
Always choose to see the funny side

DESIRE:
To live for the moment and enjoy it

STRATEGY:
Play, make jokes, be funny

THE LOVER

MOTTO:
I only have eyes for you

DESIRE:
Intimacy through sensual pleasure

STRATEGY:
Be attractive, physically and
emotionally

THE MAGICIAN

MOTTO:
It can happen

DESIRE:
To know how the universe works

STRATEGY:
Develop a vision and live it

THE OUTLAW

MOTTO:
Rules are meant to be broken

DESIRE:
Revenge or revolution

STRATEGY:
Disrupt and destroy

THE REGULAR GUY

MOTTO:
All men and women are created equal

DESIRE:
Connection with others

STRATEGY:
Develop ordinary, solid virtues.
The common touch

THE RULER

MOTTO:
Power isn't everything,
it's the only thing

DESIRE:
Control

STRATEGY:
To exert leadership

THE SAGE

MOTTO:
The truth will set you free

DESIRE:
The discovery of truth

STRATEGY:
To understand and reflect on oneself

When you find yourself trapped in the Forest, try looking at the problem through these different eyes. If you are working in a group, divide into twos and threes and take one or two archetypes each and see what new paths you can find.

There are just three steps to using the Headhunting tool:
1. **Write out the Defined Problem.**
2. **Choose an archetype from the Headhunting list.**
3. **Imagine how the archetype would view and approach the problem.**

The Desert

It's easy to become seduced by a mirage in the desert. In fact it takes a degree of courage to ignore the spurious promise of a solution that almost works.

But in our heart of hearts, we always know when something is a waste of time. At best it is going to be a second-rate solution to the problem, one that never gives us the satisfaction of an "Aha!" moment.

Our reluctance to walk away is compounded by the fact that the steps we took to bring the mirage into view were logical and made perfect sense. So why turn around?

My advice would be don't dwell on it, just do it.

The Backtracking tool makes it easy.

I've seen this approach to creative problem-solving in a number of different forms. But essentially it requires you to look at the thought process within the problem and go against its flow.

Here's an example that dates back to the early years of the last century in New York. It's a simple problem and the solution affects us all to this day.

Here it is:

A high-rise building has an elevator that is very slow. Since the building was erected, technology has advanced and other buildings in the neighborhood have elevators that are much faster. So the residents are dissatisfied. They don't like to wait. And some of them have decided to leave and move to a newer building to avoid the inconvenience. This has worried the landlords who know that they cannot install a faster elevator. It would be too expensive and disruptive. What are they to do?

The mirage that immediately pops up will, in most cases, suggest you do something about the elevator.

Is it possible to reprogram the elevator to ensure it doesn't stop unnecessarily? Does the building employ a bellboy to ensure a more efficient operation? Is it possible to put a new elevator on the outside of the building? This might be cheaper and cause less disruption to the residents. In peak hours, does the elevator stop at fewer floors encouraging the residents to walk a couple of flights?

There are many less than satisfactory solutions that involve the elevator. So let's backtrack to the problem and see if we can head off in the opposite direction. A succinct version of the problem, from the landlords' point of view, might be:

"Tenants are leaving the building because the elevator is too slow."

That makes the elevator the problem.

But if we restate this and decide to make the tenants the problem, it would look something like this.

"The tenants hate waiting for the elevator."

The principle of Backtracking is to get to the core of the problem and state it backward. We can do this by putting "not" in front of verbs or substituting antonyms where possible. In our simple example the problem after Backtracking might be:

"The tenants love waiting for the elevator." Or it could be:

"The elevator loves waiting for the tenants."

If we can make sense of one of these statements, we might find a new route through the Desert.

In the case of the Manhattan elevator it's the notion that the tenants might love waiting that solves the problem. The landlords put mirrors in the foyer and beside the lifts on each floor. The tenants stopped worrying about their waiting time when they could spend it adjusting their ties and admiring their hair. It's a design feature that has been adopted by architects all over the world.

Edward de Bono describes a similar technique he calls the "Intermediate Impossible." In his example the challenge is to stop factories that are built on rivers polluting the towns that are downstream from them.

He worked with the statement, "The factories should be downstream of themselves." As absurd as this may sound, it led to the idea of mandating that factory inlet pipes must be downstream of their outlet pipes. If the factories pollute the water, they will be the first to suffer.

There are only two steps to using the Backtracking tool.

1. **State and restate the problem.**
2. **Explore statements that state the exact reverse or opposite of the problem.**

The other way out of the Desert is with a group activity we call "Storming."

It's a version of Brainstorming but with a twist. It uses a very similar process. Unfortunately, few people are properly taught how to brainstorm, so this is an opportune moment to look at the rules.

Brainstorming was introduced in 1953 by Alex Osborn in his book *Applied Imagination*. He was working with senior executives who had become stuck in a rut and wanted to find fresh approaches to problems within their organizations.

As much as it looks like a scatterbrain process, it works more effectively if the following disciplines are followed.

1. **Send your ego away for the day. It is not a competition.**
2. **Stay in the room, not in your head. Just listen and respond.**
3. **Never say no, say maybe.**
4. **Don't hesitate and hold back.**
5. **Don't refine or perfect your ideas. Just say them.**
6. **Don't be too serious. Humor sparks creativity.**
7. **Write everything down. Everything.**
8. **Don't steer the conversation. Go with the flow.**
9. **Set a time limit and work in bursts.**
10. **Set a quota and struggle to get there.**

Rule number two is the hardest to follow. "Just listen and respond." Most of us are too self-conscious to do this. (Particularly if some people in the group aren't following rule number one!) We judge ourselves and second-guess the judgments of others in the room who are listening.

This kills spontaneity.

To get over this we sometimes do an exercise called "Orchestra Cacophonica."

Before the session we ask everyone to bring a "sound generator." This is anything that can make a sound they can control. It could be a tin with a marble in it. It could be a musical instrument. Anything at all. The only rule is that if you can play the instrument, you can't use it. You have to swap it with someone else. We want no musical ability in the room.

We then set this exercise. We ask everyone to close their eyes and, using only their "sound generators," tell the following story.

"It's a beautiful sunny day and you are walking in the park. The sky is blue and the birds are singing. And then suddenly the weather changes. Clouds form and it starts to rain. As the rain gathers force you run for the cover of the trees and shelter there during the storm. And then, just as suddenly, the skies clear, the sun shines and the birds start singing again. You continue your walk on this perfect summer's day."

The first attempt is usually ample justification for the name "Orchestra Cacophonica." But on the second attempt you'll start to hear and feel something meaningful. Through spontaneity and interaction, by carefully listening and responding, even the most corporate group will find themselves telling this simple story in sound.

It's a great experience for all involved and it promotes a sense of collaboration and openness that will dramatically improve the brainstorming session that follows.

When I ask people in workshops to tell me the rules of brainstorming
they usually say (sometimes rather wearily), "There are no bad ideas."
That seems to be the only principle that has survived the 50-odd years
since Alex Osborn unveiled this powerful tool.

And it's nonsense. There are plenty of bad ideas. More bad than good,
probably. The point is to acknowledge that bad ideas can lead to good
ideas. They are stepping stones.

And that is where Storming plays a role.

When we conduct a Storming session we are looking for bad ideas. The worse the
better. We follow the rules of a classic brainstorming session. We encourage exactly
the same behavior—spontaneity, humor, and a lack of self-involvement. We work
in bursts of 20–30 minutes and set a target figure for the number of bad ideas we
want to see written up on the board. We write them all down.

In these sessions it's always easy to maintain a high level of energy and involvement.
Looking for bad ideas is very disinhibiting. Suddenly no one is worrying if their ideas
are bad! Or if they are looking bad. It's very hard to look bad in a Storming session.

This makes it a very effective tool for escaping the Desert. The mirage is obliterated
by a storm of atrocious, ridiculous, counter-productive suggestions.

But what's interesting is that these suggestions are all a response to the problem. As
bad as they may be, they are always relevant. They are always connected to the issue
we are trying to resolve. And when we harvest these ideas at the end of each burst
we find we can often use the alchemy of our imagination to transform them into
something useful.

In fact it is sometimes easier to create a great idea out of a terrible one than
it is to make a good idea out of something that is merely mediocre.

There are four steps to using the Storming tool:
1. **Write out the Defined Problem.**
2. **"Storm" bad ideas for 20-30 minutes.**
3. **Select the most provocative.**
4. **Reverse the thinking to find a positive idea.**

The City

Complexity can paralyze creative thinking. When we get overloaded
with information we get stuck in the City.

This often happens when we know a problem inside-out. We know too much.
They say the curse of a wise man is that he can see and understand both sides of
an argument. The curse of the City is that you can see as many reasons for not
doing something as for doing it. The push and pull of so many conflicting thoughts
eventually leads to a mental gridlock and our ideas stop flowing.

The way forward is to simplify your understanding of the
problem. The Ideascape has two tools for doing that—
Sidewalking and Lollipopping.

Sidewalking, as the name suggests, is when you take your thoughts along a parallel
path. How often have you been stuck in heavy traffic and thought it would be
quicker to get out and walk?

Sidewalking lets you do that by finding analogies.
This is a conscious decision to find the sort of Triggers we observed in Chapter 5.

Gutenberg's observation of the wine press was an inadvertent moment
of Sidewalking. Similarly the ballpoint pen and the roll-on deodorant
lived in parallel universes. Both used a ball to dispense fluid onto a
surface. Few people realize that one inspired the other.

In Berkeley University in California, the engineering faculty has developed a super
wide-angle surveillance lens after studying the peripheral vision of a fly's eye.

At the Marine Science Center of Northeastern University, Joseph Ayers has created
the Robolobster. It's a mineseeker that combs the ocean floor by mimicking the
movements of a lobster as it searches for food.

In advertising, it's very common to see a good idea in one category resurface in
an entirely different category. This is very much a part of the Procter and Gamble
philosophy. They called it "Search and Reapply." The differences in style and
execution usually disguise the similarity of the underlying concepts.

In Sidewalking we set out to do this very deliberately.

McDonald's in Australia were looking for inspiration to improve the service in their Drive-thru restaurants. Where did they look? They spent a day with the pit crews at a motor racing circuit outside Sydney.

The process is very simple.

Look at the attributes and methods within your problem, much as we did with Trailblazing, and then see if you can find ones that are similar in other, unrelated activities.

For example, imagine you are a telephone company that wants to give a free cellphone service to teenagers. This will instill long-term loyalty to your brand and provide a real value to the community as these children will always be able to make a call if they are in some sort of difficulty.

But how do you cover the cost? Telephone payment plans are increasingly complex and most teenagers can't afford them.

Look for an analogy. What other medium gives its services away free? Television. Trade magazines. Radio.

How do they fund it? Advertising revenue. So how could we introduce advertising into free telephone calls to cover the cost? A blipvert every five minutes that lasts only five seconds? An advertising text message at the end of every call?

This is a crude example but it shows how we can move from an area where our thoughts are congested by knowing too much to an area where our thoughts flow freely because we don't know much at all. But the thoughts we have in this parallel world are relevant to our problem and may well lead to a usable idea.

Sidewalking requires just three simple steps.

1. Define the attributes of the problem.

2. Find similar attributes in an unrelated activity.

3. See if what works for one can work for the other.

The other way out of the City is to simplify the problem by recruiting the services of our Inner Child.

> I've called this tool Lollipopping after the "Lollipop Ladies" in the UK. These are crossing guards, usually women, who use a lollipop-shaped sign to halt the traffic as they help school children across the road.

> Lollipopping is a set of exercises that help us regress to our childhood and see the problem through innocent eyes. This helps reduce complexity and put us in touch with a part of ourselves that is curious, unrestrained by responsibility, and carelessly creative.

In workshops, I have found people either love or completely reject this process. Some think it's childish. It is. I think that is a good thing but I suppose it depends on how fondly your recall your childhood. Others have told me that it's the most enjoyable of the tools and one they have found very productive.

> It's certainly the least disciplined and process-driven. But there is a structure to it.

It starts with a guided visualization.

> Close your eyes and imagine you are back in a school classroom. You are seven or eight years old. Spend a few moments remembering what it felt like. Explore your senses—the look and feel of the room, how it smells, how it sounds. Remember the sounds outside the room. See and hear the other children.

Spend a minute or two revisiting and recreating this time of your life.

> Then imagine a teacher comes into the room. Using the blackboard, he or she explains the problem you are trying to solve in language you can understand. He uses no jargon, no complicated words, and no complex ideas. He just explains the problem in words a seven-year-old can understand and writes it up on the board.

Now, without talking, write the problem down as he has or she has stated it on a blank piece of paper. Then start to draw your thoughts around it. Some people find it easier to recapture their childish spirit if they use their non-dominant hand. Whichever hand you use, try and doodle your thoughts and ideas so that the process is essentially a visual one. You can use words but not sentences.

If you are working in a team, from time to time, look at other people's scribbles. I have, on a couple of occasions, come up with good ideas by completely misinterpreting someone else's drawing. It's a bit like finding faces in clouds or trees. Your imagination is conditioned by the problem you are trying to solve and finds relevant thoughts and ideas in things it doesn't quite recognize or understand.

After 20–30 minutes, review your doodles and see if your adult mind can find some sense and new ideas in them. If you've been working in a group, get everyone to make presentations back to the room explaining their work and seeing what other people see in it.

Lollipopping is a fun and liberating exercise. It encourages a stress-free exploration of the problem. This is important. Stress, anxiety, and expectations all kill creative thinking.

If we want to escape the gridlock of the city, a child's simple sense of wonder is going to be more helpful than an adult's confused and overheated sense of urgency.

Lollipopping is a four-step process:

1. Close your eyes and visualize your way back to your favorite childhood classroom.

2. Watch the teacher explain the problem you are trying to solve in childish terms.

3. Doodle your "childish" thoughts on a blank sheet of paper.

4. Review the results with your "adult" mind.

We now have eight tools for navigating the four regions of the Ideascape.

Let's take an overview and see how the process works from start to finish.

Step 1.

Define the Problem. We have ten modules in Chapter 6 that you can use to get from a Perceived Problem to a Defined Problem.

Step 2.

Find out where we are in the Ideascape. If we get stuck while trying to find a solution, we need to know where we are stuck so that we can choose an appropriate tool to get our minds working again.

Step 3.

Experiment with one or both of the tools that are assigned to the particular region in which we are stuck.

If we are in the Ocean, try Fishing or Diving.
If we are in the Forest, try Trailblazing or Headhunting.
If we are in the Desert, try Backtracking or Storming.
If we are in the City, try Sidewalking or Lollipopping.

Step 4.

Write everything down and pray for good luck.

I sometimes ask myself if Ideascape is a process or a system.

According to my dictionary, a system is defined as "a group of interacting, interrelated, or interdependent elements forming a complex whole."

On that basis, it might be better to call the Ideascape a system.

The same dictionary defines a process as "a series of actions, changes, or functions bringing about a result."

That doesn't seem too far off the mark either.

But I'm reluctant to call the Ideascape a process as I'm always aware of Step 4—the need for good luck. And I like to think that a process is not dependent on something so unpredictable and capricious.

I'll leave you to decide.

One thing I do know. Creating a wonderful, novel, and usable idea is not the end of the process in solving a problem.

It's closer to the start.

What remains now is to make sure that idea is turned into action.

10. Creativity at work: How to build an Ideas Culture

Innovation is a three-stage process.

First, find a problem. Pursue a philosophy of "constructive dissatisfaction" and identify those areas where you could change something and improve it.

The second stage is creative and this is where the Ideascape can help. Pull the problem apart, subject it to the most painstaking, 360-degree examination and then generate ideas that will lead to new and better solutions. Unfortunately, an idea is only an idea. It doesn't become an innovation until it is put into practice.

Stage three is the real challenge—making it happen. If we don't have an effective process for implementing our ideas, then the thrill of our creative endeavors may well turn to disappointment and eventually disillusionment. We'll wonder why we bothered. And if this happens repeatedly, we'll stop bothering.

Creative people cannot survive in an environment that does not nurture and support them. They stop being creative.

I saw this frequently while I was working in advertising agencies. I'd employ someone with an excellent resumé and wonderful ideas in their portfolio and then mistakenly assign them to a team that was producing mediocre work. My hope was that they'd raise the standard and improve the team. Sadly, the reverse would usually happen. The new recruit's creativity would wither in that environment and he or she would start to produce lackluster and predictable ideas.

The obverse would also prove to be true. I'd move someone who was producing fairly average work into a creative team and they'd flourish and start to deliver fresh and interesting ideas. There's one simple lesson I learned from this:

Culture is the key to creativity and innovation.

And culture is the responsibility of management. Creativity may sometimes be the work of an individual but innovation is always the work of a team led by management.

This subject is really worthy of a whole book. And a mountain of excellent books has been written. (I've listed some of them in the Bibliography.) Were you to climb that mountain, I think you'd return with Ten Commandments that are fundamental to building an innovation culture.

The Tablet Of Stone

1. Management must lead by example.

If innovation is going to work it must become a philosophy that permeates every level of the organization. Ideas are fragile and so are the feelings of the people who create them. If the management team does not fully and visibly embrace the need for "constructive dissatisfaction" and the desire for positive change, the rest of the company will shy away from the challenge.

It's not sufficient for the management team to set an innovation agenda and then sit back and act as the arbiters and judges of the ideas that are presented. The management must invest its own time, creativity, and energy in the process.

2. Goals must be set.

Some companies operate a "suggestion box" process of innovation. The virtue of this is that it encourages everyone to know they have a voice. They can express their ideas in the belief that they will be relayed to the people in charge. They can even do it anonymously.

But the overwhelming problem with this system, however well-intended, is that it lacks focus. Once the suggestion box is full, it's unmanageable. True, there may be a few excellent suggestions. And some may see the light of day. But that still means the majority of the ideas will be neglected and undeveloped as there will be insufficient time and resources to act effectively on so many different and unconnected issues. And so it follows, the majority of contributors will feel their efforts were worthless. That's a downward spiral and one that will kill the staff's enthusiasm.

But if a goal is set, it acts as a funnel. Everyone's contributions will be relevant as they have been inspired by the same objectives and desired outcome. It's by narrowing the focus that we broaden the involvement of the staff. Everyone can feel they played a valuable role. Everyone is a part of the process. And even a plethora of ideas remains manageable. That is an upward spiral.

3. Roles and responsibilities must be established.

As well as being a philosophy, innovation is a process. It's complex, time-consuming, and therefore expensive. If it's going to happen, it needs to be organized and controlled. That means someone needs to be given the responsibility and the necessary powers.

As there are many stages to the process, it's more likely to be a team but it must not develop into a separate department. Innovation needs to be a cross-disciplinary function and one that operates in all departments.

When members of the staff have an idea, they need to know where they can take it. The first port of call needs to be someone who can ensure that an idea gets into the funnel.

4. Teams must be multi-disciplinary.

The staffing of an innovation team needs to be very carefully considered as there are many diverse roles that need to be filled.

IDEO's Tom Kelley, in his book *The Ten Faces of Innovation*, organizes these roles into such categories as Anthropologists, who contribute insights by observing human behavior; Experimenters, who try new things; Hurdlers, who surmount obstacles; Collaborators, who bring people together and get things done; and Caregivers, who anticipate and meet customer needs.

Overall, the team needs to contain what Ned Herrmann would describe as a Whole Brain. His HBDI profiling system is a very good tool for ensuring that an innovation team has the necessary thinking preferences to function well.

LOVES FACTS
Excels at analyzing data
Is extremely logical

LOVES IDEAS
Excels at imagination and innovation
Sees the big picture

LOVES PROCESS
Excels at organization
Is highly detailed and systematic

LOVES PEOPLE
Excels at intuition
Is caring and highly expressive

This diagram looks at how the roles fit into the four quadrants of his system. While the team needs to collaborate well, it doesn't need to be like-minded.

Jerry Hirschberg, in his book *The Creative Priority*, looks at the value of what he calls "Creative Abrasion." It's the differences in the way people think that often stimulates new and interesting ideas. People who think in the same way are likely to agree and support one another. But people who approach a subject from different perspectives are more likely to challenge one another. It's in that challenge that we find Koestler's "intersection of two matrices of thought."

5. Resources must be allocated.

The management team must invest in the innovation process—time, money, and space. Some companies, Google for example, encourage their staff to dedicate a fixed percentage of their working week to innovation. In so doing, the management team has generated a high level of motivation by demonstrating its commitment to both the staff and the process. Clearly it believes that this investment will be more than repaid by the value of these initiatives to the company.

I once worked in an agency where the last Friday of every month was a designated "Idea Friday." It was a significant investment of resources. But as well as providing an opportunity for ideation, it proved that innovation was an opportunity for everyone to play a role in the development of the company.

As well as allowing for the investment of working hours, a budget needs to be assigned to cover development costs. Some ideas need funding. The concept may require research or prototyping before it can be evaluated. The team needs to know how far they can take the idea to investigate its potential. And that means knowing how much the management team is prepared to spend. They need a figure.

Lastly, space needs to be provided. Creative thinking requires access to a different headspace and working in a different physical space can help. Our imagination is susceptible to priming. A comfortable room that removes us from the habitual thinking of the workplace is liberating and encourages us to think differently. Just going there puts us in the right frame of mind.

6. Values must come from the top.

It is the management's responsibility to create a risk-free environment for creativity and innovation. People need to feel secure. Only then will they experiment with their ideas and share them with colleagues in a spirit of collaboration.

Fear of ridicule kills spontaneity. And yet we must learn to embrace the absurd, the irrational, and the crazy thoughts that drive the creative process. Einstein once said,

> "If at first the idea is not absurd, then there is no hope for it!"

This poses one of the greatest challenges to building an innovation culture. But if an innovation program is to succeed, everyone involved must feel that his or her position in the company is not compromised by making a suggestion that seems ridiculous.

Managing negative criticism is a large part of instilling the correct values. It comes in many forms—knee-jerk rejection, damning with faint praise, laughter, or even silence.

Tom Kelley warns against its most insidious practitioner, the man who starts his response and analysis with the words, "Being the Devil's advocate for a moment…." This gives license to a highly destructive critique for which the devil and not the speaker will allegedly take responsibility.

Only the management team can demonstrate the behavior that defines the company culture. They must actively participate in the innovation process and submit their own ideas for collaborative development. They must take the same risks and expose the same vulnerabilities as the rest of the company if they are to lead by example.

7. Communication must be constant.

Every member of the company needs to know why they should devote time to an activity that is probably not in their job description.

The management team needs to explain why a strategy of innovation is going to develop the company and benefit the people who work there. And then they need to keep an open line of communication through which they report on all developments and outcomes of the program. Innovation is an ongoing process and there needs to be a constant level of communication to reflect and reinforce that.

8. Evaluation must be transparent.

The only way to ensure that people feel their ideas are going to receive a fair hearing is to establish a clear process and set of criteria for judgment. This will differ from business to business. Gut reaction always plays a part in assessing a new idea. But there must be a more rigorous and less subjective process to follow.

Everyone involved in the innovation program must know it, understand it, and believe it to be fair.

9. Success must be rewarded and celebrated.

Creative cultures thrive on a loop of constant feedback—goals are set, progress is monitored and reported, results are announced, accolades and rewards are given, the new ideas are implemented, and then new goals are set. And around we go. This cycle of positive energy is like a flywheel that maintains momentum.

It's important to recognize and reward the key proponents of an innovation. Rewards build motivation and commitment to the project and encourage others to follow the example.

But it's important to remember the role that culture plays. For that reason it's important to celebrate throughout the company. This creates a sense of involvement and shared responsibility and ownership and helps spread the commitment and motivation.

10. Implementation must be swift.

Ideas have a shelf life. They go stale quite quickly. And sometimes an idea can start to feel old before it's had the chance to develop and become an innovation.

This is a tragic waste of creative energy. Once an idea has been approved it must be acted upon immediately or scheduled to happen within a stated timeframe.

If this doesn't happen, the idea will probably die of neglect. It will fade away.

But it won't be forgotten entirely. An idea will always be remembered by the team who burned the midnight oil. It will serve as a daily reminder that the management team did not deliver on their side of the bargain. This can undermine the staff's confidence in an innovation program and is extremely demoralizing.

Admittedly, some great ideas come before their time. But if the management team decides to shelve an idea it must communicate the reasons swiftly and fully to all concerned. That is the only way of stopping disappointment turning into disillusionment.

Remember the Ten Commandments for an Innovation Culture:
1. **Management must lead by example.**
2. **Goals must be set.**
3. **Roles and responsibilities must be established.**
4. **Teams must be multi-disciplinary.**
5. **Resources must be allocated.**
6. **Values must come from the top.**
7. **Communication must be constant.**
8. **Evaluation must be transparent.**
9. **Success must be rewarded and celebrated.**
10. **Implementation must be swift.**

11. Conclusion

I hope that, if you have reached this page of the book, a few key themes and messages will have emerged.

The world is changing. Evolution is accelerating. If we are going to survive and thrive we need to harness our creativity and find new ways of doing the things we do. We can all be a part of the process. Each of us is born with a relentlessly active imagination. Learning to apply it is a skill, not a gift. Anyone can learn how. I know I did.

While there may be no such thing as a creative process, there are processes that lead us closer to the Trigger, our moment of inspiration. That is the role the Ideascape plays. Try it the next time you are suffering "Thinker's Block." It won't give you an answer, but it will point you in the right direction. It'll help you break out of the box.

And if you get lucky and happen upon a great idea, then treat it with care. Ideas are very fragile. They should only be exposed in an environment where they will be nurtured, developed, and made to happen.

Index

Bibliography

Lateral Logic Puzzles, Erwin Brecher, Sterling
How to Mind Map, Tony Buzan, HarperCollins
Mind Maps at Work, Tony Buzan, Plume
The Mind Assault Course, Dave Chatten and Carolyn Skitt, Carlton Books
Creativity, Mihaly Csikszentmihalyi, Harper Perennial
Flow, Mihaly Csikszentmihalyi, Harper & Row
Po: Beyond Yes and No, Edward de Bono, Penguin
Six Thinking Hats, Edward de Bono, Penguin
Faster, James Gleick, Vintage
The Creative Brain, Ned Herrmann, Ned Herrmann Group
The Whole Brain Business Book, Ned Herrmann, McGraw-Hill
The Creative Priority, Jerry Hirshberg, Collins
The Ten Faces of Innovation, Tom Kelley, Currency

The Act of Creation, Arthur Koestler, Penguin
The Hero and the Outlaw, Margaret Mark and Carol Pearson, McGraw-Hill
Quick-to-Solve Brainteasers, J.J. Mendoza Fernandez, Sterling
Archimedes' Bathtub, David Perkins, W.W. Norton
Zen and the Art of Motorcycle Maintenance, Robert Pirsig, Bantam
Tricky Lateral Thinking Puzzles, Paul Sloane and Des MacHale, Sterling
The Dynamics of Creation, Anthony Storr, Ballantine Books

Acknowledgments

The author would like to thank Kieran Ots, Glen McNab, and Simon Cave for their fantastic work on designing the CD-ROM that accompanies this book.